dark horses

AN ANTHOLOGY EDITED BY

Joy Katz and Kevin Prufer

UNIVERSITY OF ILLINOIS PRESS   URBANA AND CHICAGO

dark horses

POETS ON OVERLOOKED POEMS

Library of Congress Cataloging-in-Publication Data
Dark horses : poets on overlooked poems : an anthology /
edited by Joy Katz & Kevin Prufer.
p.   cm.
Includes bibliographical references and index.
ISBN-13: 978-0-252-03053-6 (cloth : alk. paper)
ISBN-10: 0-252-03053-2 (cloth : alk. paper)
ISBN-13: 978-0-252-07287-1 (pbk. : alk. paper)
ISBN-10: 0-252-07287-1 (pbk. : alk. paper)
1. English poetry. 2. American poetry.
I. Katz, Joy, 1963– II. Prufer, Kevin.
PR1175.D2714   2005
821.008—dc22   2005013683

contents

Introduction

DARK HORSES began as a conversation among poets about wonderful, obscure poems we'd come across over the years. There were five of us sitting in a dim Italian restaurant in Kansas City, talking about odd poems we recalled from defunct literary journals and gems that had turned up in library books that hadn't been checked out in years. These poems shone through the gloom of forgotten authors and out-of-print magazines, to say nothing of the overwhelming number of poems we read each year in literary journals and slim volumes. What struck us most about that evening wasn't so much the poets mentioned—we knew almost nothing about many of them—but the pleasure and excitement we all felt talking about their work.

We couldn't wait to round up these pieces and send them to each other. Partly it was the joy and pride of a great sighting, as if the poems were near-extinct birds. Partly it was how helpless they seemed gathering dust in library storerooms or moldering beneath stacks of journals in used bookstores. After all, as practitioners of an esoteric art, our own work would probably become extinct one day (as Billy Collins points out in these pages).

Over the next few months, two of us kept the conversation going. If each of us recalled at least one splendid, overlooked poem, we wondered, how many other poets did? And what would such a collection be like? We sent form letters to some hundred poets asking each for an unknown or underappreciated poem written by anyone, in any language, from any era. We hoped to include experimental poets and formalists, poets within and outside the academy, poets emerging and established, poets from far-ranging backgrounds. Our idea was that these potential contributors would begin with a little archaeological work, bringing to light poems that our readers, who would be both poets and fans of poetry, could enjoy and would be unlikely to find anywhere else. We also asked them to prepare a short essay or bit of discussion about the poem or poet.

In all, sixty-seven came through. Some contributors told us they'd spent years promoting a poet's work among their friends or publishers to no avail. Others sent six or seven poems. A few made special trips to rare-book rooms in university libraries to copy poems they'd discovered while working on other projects. We received piles of poems we had never read, many by writers whose names were new to us. Some offerings were contemporary, others hundreds of years old. Reading the submissions was like being back in that restaurant, but with dozens of poets at the table—poets from different worlds, with different predilections, each with something compelling to offer.

Right away we realized we couldn't organize the book by tradition or literary period, since the poems came from too many different traditions and periods. Clearly, *Dark Horses* would be a kind of orchestrated clamor. Like our original conversation, the poems would be united by the ardor and enthusiasm of their promoters.

Of course, we never meant *Dark Horses* to compete with the big anthologies such as Norton, Oxford, or Cambridge. But as we worked, we realized that those volumes have come to define even wildly prolific poets by the five or six poems that the editors select—poems that might better serve as a rough outline of a poet's work. Poets who wrote in many different styles over decades end up simplified, made less complex, and the same poems appear over and over. (About a decade ago, the poet and editor William Harmon compiled a collection, *The Top 500 Poems,* consulting every other anthology in print to determine the 500 most frequently represented poems, concluding that they are the ones our culture prizes most. Blake's "The Tyger" was voted Most Valuable Poem.)

But frequency of publication doesn't define a poem's beauty, power, or ambition. In fact, we thought, being overplayed on the poetic hit parade can hasten a poem's demise. No matter the reason, many of the really fine poems by any great poet are never included in the textbook anthologies. And given the credentials that living poets need to make it into big anthologies—a major prize or two, a stellar publication record, the support of the academy—most never see their work inscribed in those pages.

It's no surprise, then, that a number of poems in *Dark Horses* were written by poets on the fringe of literary society. Some work (or worked) in other fields: Ed Barrett teaches at the Massachusetts Institute of Technology's media lab. F. T. Prince was a contemporary of W. H. Auden, but he lived an isolated life in Southampton, far from the bluster of the poetry scenes in New York and London. Likewise, Joseph Ceravolo, a little-studied figure of the New York School, lived a quiet life with his family. Some poets included here are better known as other kinds of writers: the literary critic R. P. Blackmur, the novelist Kingsley Amis, the Dada artist Man Ray.

We received poems by poets who are as of this writing all but unknown to most readers despite having published widely—Eleanor Ross Taylor, for instance, who lives in Virginia, and Norman Pritchard, a New Yorker whose books slipped out of the poetry conversation sometime in the '70s. James Still published many books, but he was pigeonholed as an Appalachian poet and was barely known outside the region.

If there is any larger category here, it is poems by poets whose body of work is small—a possible commentary on the market value of being prolific. Charlotte Mew, lauded by Virginia Woolf and Thomas Hardy, published just one book, as did the much-praised Naomi Lazard. The World War I soldier-poet John Allan Wyeth wrote a single volume that was never noticed, even during his lifetime. Some of these poets published little because they died young. In 1973, shortly after his first book was published, Thomas James committed suicide; Mew poisoned herself in 1913. Bert Meyers died of lung cancer, Adam Hammer in a car accident.

We also include rarely seen poems by authors whose work any reader will recognize. Walt Whitman's "Time to Come" hints at a still-to-be-written *Leaves of Grass* while offering a glimpse of his early, more sentimental self. An Amy Lowell poem is redeemed from the purgatory of Ezra Pound's summary dismissal. John Berryman's "Young Woman's Song," like other poems of his, is overshadowed by *77 Dream Songs*. The two Emily Dickinson poems here have been neglected by scholars and critics alike.

Our contributors turned in a motley mix of screeds, personal stories, and more scholarly investigations. Sometimes they act as Virgilian guides to the pleasures of difficult work and sometimes as frank admirers. Some share a bit of the life story of obscure characters; others provide close readings. Some introducers chose poems that were overlooked for political reasons, so politics became a part of their introductions. J. D. McClatchy writes of A. E. Housman's longtime lover Moses Jackson, and Nick Carbó discusses postcolonialism in his introduction to the Filipino poet Rafael Zulueta da Costa. There are also personal comments. Some poems influenced writers at an important point in their careers. Denise Duhamel latched on to a chatty, theatrical Ron Koertge poem in high school, before she knew she wanted to be a poet. At eighteen, Cole Swensen discovered a Seifu poem that gave her a sense of what it's like to be old. Toi Derricotte's selection comes from the first workshop she ever took, in 1968 in New York.

We hope *Dark Horses* is as delightful as it is surprising to read page by page. It is intended, most of all, to be a collection of fine work introduced by fine poets. Our contributors have selected and talked about the poems because they've remembered them for years and loved them as long. If, as a result, a few of these poems or their makers come back into the conversation—or enter it for the first time—we would be pleased. They deserve it.

4

A Bookshop Idyll

KINGSLEY AMIS

Between the *gardening* and the *cookery*
    Comes the brief *Poetry* shelf;
By the Nonesuch Donne, a thin anthology
    Offers itself.

Critical, and with nothing else to do,
    I scan the Contents page,
Relieved to find the names are mostly new;
    No one my age.

Like all strangers, they divide by sex:
    Landscape Near Parma
Interests a man, so does *The Double Vortex,*
    So does *Rilke and Buddha.*

'I travel, you see,' 'I think' and 'I can read'
    These titles seem to say;
But *I Remember You, Love is my Creed,*
    Poem for J.,

The ladies' choice, discountenance my patter
    For several seconds;
From somewhere in this (as in any) matter
    A moral beckons.

Should poets bicycle-pump the human heart
    Or squash it flat?
Man's love is of man's life a thing apart;
    Girls aren't like that.

We men have got love well weighed up; our stuff
    Can get by without it.
Women don't seem to think that's good enough;
    They write about it,

And the awful way their poems lay them open
    Just doesn't strike them.
Women are really much nicer than men:
    No wonder we like them.

Deciding this, we can forget those times
    We sat up half the night
Chock-full of love, crammed with bright thoughts, names, rhymes,
    And couldn't write.

RACHEL HADAS ON KINGSLEY AMIS' A Bookshop Idyll

Kingsley Amis' "A Bookshop Idyll" was published in his 1956 volume of verse, *A Case of Samples,* and then promptly anthologized by Donald Hall, Robert Pack, and Louis Simpson in their 1957 anthology *The New Poets of England and America.* So one can't claim that Amis' delightful poem has languished in total obscurity. Besides, even if the poem is relatively obscure, Amis is a well known author. Or is he? It's as a novelist that he's best known, and an alarming number of his wonderful novels are now out of print. Try your own bookshop idyll, and you'll find that Martin Amis has edged his father almost entirely off the fiction shelf (*Lucky Jim,* that cocky survivor, is a happy exception). And if you turn to the poetry section, you'll be unlikely to run across *A Case of Samples, A Look Round the Estate,* or *Collected Poems 1944–1979.* The three collections of poetry Amis edited may be a bit easier to find: *The New Oxford Book of Light Verse, The Faber Popular Reciter,* and the matchless (but, yes, out of print) *Amis Anthology.* So much for my justification for exhuming this poem.

But of course the poem is its own justification. It is crisp and rueful, knowing about both life and letters, wise and funny and shapely—not a word too long or short. For the browsing speaker (or rather mental soliloquizer), the bookshop offers a microcosmic map of human experience: "Between the *gardening* and the *cookery* / Comes the brief *Poetry* shelf." It's to poetry that the speaker is drawn; he sounds almost bored, but the casual tone is deceptive. How could it not be, given that what we are reading is after all a poem?

Critical, and with nothing else to do,
    I scan the Contents page,
Relieved to find the names are mostly new;
    No one my age.

Exactly captured here is the feeling any poet has when opening an anthology. The next observation follows: "Like all strangers, they divide by sex." This perception also rings true. When we encounter other people, or even hear of the birth of a new baby, gender is just about the first thing we notice or ask about. But applying this human trait to the realm of poetry gives a fresh twist to the latter—fresh in the sense that Amis the poet, no less than Amis the novelist, pays close attention to how people act, and we his readers benefit from his sharp eyes.

But there's more to this gender business than the striking fact that poems as well as people divide along those lines. Ten or fifteen years after "A Bookshop Idyll" first appeared, it became objectionable in many quarters to say men and women were essentially different; later on, the terms of the argument were reversed, and it became offensive to say the opposite. We are now living in a time when anthologies are devised to appeal to every conceivable segment of the market: male, female, gay, straight, feline, canine. I would love to hear Amis' response to *Queer Pup*, an anthology of dog poems exclusively by gay poets.

Back to the simpler subdivisions in "A Bookshop Idyll." The browser muses that poems by men—poems with titles like "Landscape near Parma," "The Double Vortex," "Rilke and Buddha"—announce "'I travel, you see,' 'I think' and 'I can read.' The poems by women have titles like "I Remember You," "Love is My Creed," and "Poem for J." The larger contrast suggested here is limned with economy and wit:

. . . somewhere in this (as in any) matter
    A moral beckons.

Should poets bicycle-pump the human heart
    Or squash it flat?
Man's love is of man's life a thing apart;
    Girls aren't like that.

We men have got love well weighed up; our stuff
    Can get by without it.
Women don't seem to think that's good enough;
    They write about it . . .

That "bicycle-pump," funny in itself, is even better because it's jux-taposed with a pumped-up line silently borrowed from Donna Julia's farewell letter to Juan in the first Canto of *Don Juan:*

> Man's love is of man's life a thing apart,
>   Tis women's whole existence

a sentiment which, in turn, Byron is reported to have extracted from Madame de Stael: thus male Amis incorporates into a poem musing on gender differences in poetry a line from a male poet impersonating a female character—a line ultimately derived from a female writer.

The rest of the "Idyll" edges away from letters back toward life, or rather to the confused tangle of the two in the arena of love poetry ham-pered by or deprived of love, and, possibly, the reverse. The poem ends by recalling

>   those times
>   We sat up half the night
> Chock-full of love, crammed with bright thoughts, names, rhymes,
>   And couldn't write.

Amis deftly fits so many ideas and observations, general and specif-ic—about the sexes, publishing, poetry, and even just standing leafing through a book while in one's mind a notion sneakily beckons—into thirty-six casually tight lines that I always remember this poem as longer than it really is. Perhaps the "Idyll" of the title recalls the Theocritean world of pastoral—the pastorals of love, of books, of poetry, of compet-ing swains singing their love songs. And the pastoral, with its restricted space, is a miniaturizing genre. The poem could easily be fleshed out into a short story, as is also the case with many better-known poems by Amis' lifelong friend, Philip Larkin.

Larkin, who wrote two novels before devoting himself exclusively to poetry, once said that novels are about other people while poems are about oneself. But his work, and Amis', too, proves that that distinc-tion isn't fair to poetry. "A Bookshop Idyll" may need to be superficially revised in a Barnes and Noble or Amazon world, but people haven't changed. Deborah Tannen's best-selling book from the early '90s, *You Just Don't Understand Me: Men and Women in Conversation,* was, I read somewhere, required reading in a Congressional committee in the wake of the Clarence Thomas/Anita Hill imbroglio. "A Bookshop Idyll" should be required reading for Tannen and her ilk.

from The Ridge Farm

A. R. AMMONS

15

considering mutability and muck,
transforming compositions and
decompositions, ups and downs, comings
and goings, you have, sir, passed
from a thousand orifices, some
beneath you on the evolutionary
scale: visibly moved, the gentleman
got some roll-on ban deodorant
and tried to rub me off (or out):
shit sticks: its fragrance in the old
days confirmed the caveman he was coming
home: a man's shit (or tribe's) reflects
(nasally) the physical makeup of the man
and the physiologies of those others
present, plus what they have gathered
from the environment
to pass through themselves

the odor of shit is like language,
an unmistakable assimilation of a
use, tone, flavor, accent hard to
fake: enemy shit smells like the enemy:
everything is more nearly incredible
than you thought at first

This poem is one of my guides—a copy of it faces me at my writing desk, and I use it as a reminder to be as careful as I know how with words. It also reminds me that what I think is my voice obscures what is in actuality shit—a rich and fathomless condensation of history and my ongoing life in the world. I continue to enjoy its humor and amazement: it has changed forever my experience of stink! In fact, the poem—actually one of fifty-one sections that make up a long poem in the book *Sumerian Vistas* (1987)—startles me now as much as it did when I first read it years ago.

In its first line, the realm of thinking suggested by a formal Latinate word like "mutability" is juxtaposed with the plain Middle English "muck," and the poem provokes contemplation of the relation between them, a relation characteristic of Ammons and of the meditative tradition his work embodies. It also prompts a reflection on language as a medium between meaningful lived experience and the voice, which uses language to make meaning.

Ammons was born in 1926 and grew up on a farm in eastern North Carolina. After studying science and working for a short time in business, he turned to poetry and taught for many years at Cornell. He died in 2001. In his poetry he lays the physical and emotional landscape of his origins like a template over his adopted Ithaca.

"The Ridge Farm" is not as well known as others of his long poems, and the section presented here often gets lost, both because other poems receive more attention and because its themes are elaborated more thoroughly in them. To my mind, this section is as effective as any of his short poems. What seems valuable to me is the condensation of so much that was particular to his writing—the contemplation, the provocativeness, his humor, and his attention to the dynamic in nature. All of this comes together in one poem, with notably little waste.

New Year's Poem

MARGARET AVISON

The Christmas twigs crispen and needles rattle
Along the windowledge.
      A solitary pearl
Shed from the necklace spilled at last week's party
Lies in the suety, snow-luminous plainness
Of morning, on the windowledge beside them.
And all the furniture that circled stately
And hospitable when these rooms were brimmed
With perfumes, furs, and black-and-silver
Crisscross of seasonal conversation, lapses
Into its previous largeness.
      I remember
Anne's rose-sweet gravity, and the stiff grave
Where cold so little can contain;
I mark the queer delightful skull and crossbones
Starlings and sparrows left, taking the crust,
And the long loop of winter wind
Smoothing its arc from dark Arcturus down
To the bricked corner of the drifted courtyard,
And the still windowledge.
      Gentle and just pleasure
It is, being human, to have won from space
This unchill, habitable interior
Which mirrors quietly the light
Of the snow, and the new year.

LINDA BIERDS ON MARGARET AVISON'S New Year's Poem

    I have always been drawn to poems that contain, within their meditative movements, a hint of narrative and a textured visual richness. Certainly Margaret Avison's lovely "New Year's Poem" holds that triple attraction: deeply meditative, it is a feast for the eyes, while its delicate narrative allows me to sample, again and again, a formal, seasonal party and its quiet aftermath. Still, it is not Avison's difficult balance of image, thought, and story that I most admire in "New Year's Poem": It is her remarkable achievements with structure. Using fir needles and starlings, Arcturus and a single, luminous pearl, Avison has crafted journeys: vertical, circular, concentric, diagonal, temporal, and interior.

From our position beside the poem's speaker, we follow her gaze—as we follow Avison's almost stair-stepping initial lines—down to a windowledge and a solitary pearl, a pearl that in turn has spilled down, not only from the neck of its wearer but from the past. Where has it landed? Farther down, it seems, in the suet and snow. But no, it is here, back up on the windowledge, sharing its glow with the glow of the present morning.

The pearl's vertical journey through space is mirrored twice at the poem's center, as the speaker turns her gaze from the apartment's interior down through the window to the birdclaw-etched snow, then up to Arcturus, then down once again to the courtyard, and up to the windowledge—while time shifts, as it did for the pearl, from the past of memory to the present morning. What movements we've experienced in nine lines!—from the grave to the celestial, then again, in miniature, from the skull-and-crossbones aftermath of the birds to the amber crusts of bread now lifting within their lifting bodies.

And what of those "waist" lines? Those quiet, centered moments that, taken together, echo haiku? I'm reminded once more of the birdfoot Xs etched in snow. The lines of the X, its bones, cross through one another on their diagonal journeys, each holding, for a moment, a bit of the other as they meet. So these momentary, centered lines hold a bit of the poem's past and a bit of its future. The solitary pearl cast its glow upward to illuminate the dying season and downward to blend with the opening morning. "I remember" touches the "black-and-silver crisscross" of the formal party and the enigmatic, stiff grave of another season. What a "gentle and just pleasure it is," Avison tells us, to know that a dark, cosmic-cast wind can, on occasion, smooth itself to stillness, just there at a windowledge, just there at our fingertips.

Or perhaps those compressed and centered lines, like stones dropped in a pond, create a concentric movement. This poem denies no journey. As its closing words circle back to its title, we might feel, also, that the poem's final destination has always been the interior—which has, in turn, been its point of departure: the reflective human mind, unchilled and habitable, holding simultaneously what has fallen and will fall.

Morfudd's Hair

EDWARD BARRETT

after Dafydd ap Gwilym

Now you're famous in two towns:
the one where I used to live
and your own.
I say where I used to live because
now I live only when we meet
and your cruel gold hair
comes honey and fruit.

There's a certain tact in not always killing everyone with good looks
which you must find hard to appreciate.
You bring with you a slim,
cloudless feeling of sky,
the sort of ordinary, beautiful,
clear-blue day I want to climb up a rope into,
a rope of hair let down for me alone,
looking around in disbelief,
and not tied on to anything more substantial
than a wish that counts.

You will always be someone's preference,
which feeds my bad discomfort
and my good one, the one that makes me evasive
and fun to be with you: if I try to
push you away it's phony and fateful
like fate
pushing us to discover what we can't, thanks, know
because we are it.

I see a small circle of waves in your hair when I look again.

The chargedly bright dark
when we go for a walk is the city around itself.

PAMELA ALEXANDER ON EDWARD BARRETT'S Morfudd's Hair

This poem accosted me a few years ago with its agility, its use of humor and affection to modulate something deeper. Reading it as a contemporary poem, I would say the "something" is a sadness. Unrequited love? Perhaps the old phrase comes to mind because of the poem's historical context. "Morfudd's Hair" is loosely based on part of a long poem by a Welsh poet (a contemporary, roughly, of Chaucer), who brought Provençal ideas of courtly love to Wales. So my perception of sadness is complicated by the possibility that the love in the poem reflects the conventions and idealization of those ideas. Of course, I hold both readings in my mind, as I imagine what the poet intends.

Small awkwardnesses in Barrett's poem, such as the syntax of the sentence that constitutes stanza three, feel true to the difficulty of the speaker's situation. Also deliberately awkward, the phrase "chargedly bright dark" turns out to characterize the speaker as well as the city. And in the lightness and darkness of its restrained love, the poem is wise enough to step back and look at the city, which reflects the relationship of the speaker and his beloved. The city is around itself and cannot know itself any more than its individual inhabitants can, so the poem walks away, lets us readers go.

Ed Barrett teaches and contributes to cutting-edge technical projects at the M.I.T. Media Lab, writing books with titles like *Contextual Media and Text, Con Text,* and *Hypertext: Writing with and for the Computer* alongside his poetry. His office was down the hall from mine when I taught at the Institute for many years, and I count myself lucky for that circumstance, without which it is likely I would not have met Ed or his poetry.

It seems to me that the liveliness of "Morfudd's Hair" is a fitting celebration of something important about why we need poetry. While it is contemporary in its self-conscious definitions and redefinitions, it draws inspiration from the ancient business of being human. It cuts its sentiment with humor and irony (that "certain tact"). And it has an inherent modesty. No, it says, we cannot know what we are because we are it.

Young Woman's Song

JOHN BERRYMAN

The round and smooth, my body in my bath,
If someone else would like it too.—I did,
I wanted T. to think 'How interesting'
Although I hate his voice and face, hate both.
I hate this something like a bobbing cork
Not going. I want something to hang to.—

A fierce wind roaring high up in the bare
Branches of trees,—I suppose it was lust
But it was holy and awful. All day I thought
I am a bobbing cork, irresponsible child
Loose on the waters.—What have you done at last?
A little work, a little vague chat.

I want that £3.10 hat terribly.—
What I am looking for (I *am*) may be
Happening in the gaps of what I know.
The full moon does go with you as you go.
Where am I going? I am not afraid.
Only I would be lifted lost in the flood.

<hr />

RACHEL WETZSTEON ON JOHN BERRYMAN'S Young Woman's Song

John Berryman (1914–72) is best known for his long, loosely auto-biographical poetic sequence, *The Dream Songs* (1969), in which a character named Henry—a stand-in for Berryman—broods on his life and loves, fears and follies, wanderings and woes. But Berryman wrote many other astonishing poems throughout his career, my favorite of which is a sequence of "Nervous Songs." Written mostly in 1942 and published in his first book, *The Dispossessed* (1948), these poems are narrated by a wonderfully deranged array of speakers who make Henry look like the sanest man alive: a demented priest, a mad professor, a tortured girl, a confused bridegroom, a "man forsaken and obsessed," and others.

The "Nervous Song" I love most is the first in the sequence, "Young Woman's Song." On first reading, this poem may seem more tame and straightforward than the others, but the more closely you attend to its deceptively simple language, the more rewarding Berryman's portrait of a girl on the brink of womanhood becomes.

As the poem begins, the girl is examining herself in the tub: "The round and smooth, my body in the bath." It's clear right away that she's a smart girl: the alliteration, the off-rhyme *smooth / bath,* and the mid-line caesura all attest to her strong lyrical sensibility; perhaps she's a reader of poetry. But there's more going on: the shift from "*the* round" to "*my* body" helps us see the girl's movement from aloof intellectual observation to sensual self-scrutiny—and prepares us for more examinations to come.

After admiring her pleasing shape, the young woman blurts, "If someone else would like it too"—and goes on to reveal that she has a particular young man in mind: "—I did, / I wanted T. to think 'How interesting'/ Although I hate his voice and face, hate both." Every rift of these lines is loaded with psychological ore: her defensive explosion "I did" (what imaginary nemesis said she didn't?); the abbreviation "T," which both discloses and conceals; and her stubborn repetition of "hate" (does she protest too much?) reflect the intense ambivalence of her longings.

The girl then confesses that "I hate this something like a bobbing cork / Not going. I want something to hang to." She's restless, ready to fall in love, desperate for someone to help her define herself! These lines also initiate a series of images—water, trees, moon—that give the girl's state of mind a parallel in the natural world. These images, which both unify the poem and universalize the girl's plight, continue in the second stanza, when the girl tells us of "A fierce wind roaring high up in the bare / Branches of trees,—I suppose it was lust / but it was holy and awful." She sees reflections of her confusion everywhere, but that doesn't make things any less confusing, and she wonders whether her feelings for "T." are of a sacred or profane nature. But suddenly, as if irritated by her own meditations, she cuts herself short: "—What have you done at last? / A little work, a little vague chat." Again, an imaginary interlocutor comes on the scene to accuse her of wasting her time on such childish musings.

But these musings continue in the poem's last stanza, as the young woman veers wildly (as youth does) between the guilty admission that "I want that £3.10 hat terribly," and the profound, disturbing notion that "What I am looking for (I *am*) may be / Happening in the gaps of what I know"—that life will henceforth be a difficult negotiation between heart and brain, intuition and fact. Then, perhaps startled by what she's just said, the girl becomes philosophical and coins a proverb: "The full moon does go with you as you go." In order to shed light? Cause lunacy? Both, probably: The moon, like the girl, is myriad-minded. The poem ends with the girl's bold claim that "I am not afraid. / Only I would be lifted lost in the flood." These tremendously satisfying last lines present us with a resolute if still perplexed young woman, a final bit of natural imagery (which also reminds us of the bathtub in which these thoughts take place), and some subtle paradoxes—don't we tend to think of people sinking, rather than being *lifted*, by floods? Is becoming "lost" therefore a way of finding yourself?—that reassure us that, whatever trials may await her, she's up to the challenge.

"Young Woman's Song" is a complex, beautiful, and important poem. It lets us catch Berryman in the act of trying out formal strategies (like *The Dream Songs,* "Young Woman's Song" is in three six-line, intermittently rhyming stanzas) and narrative techniques (Henry's self-knowledge is born, like the young woman's, of self-dramatization) that he will return to again and again. But it also demands our attention because it's so compelling on its own: a powerful portrait of a girl, adrift on the rough seas of adolescence, who prepares to dive, frightened but headlong, into even rougher waters ahead.

Poem

ELIZABETH BISHOP

About the size of an old-style dollar bill,
American or Canadian,
mostly the same whites, gray greens, and steel grays
—this little painting (a sketch for a larger one?)
has never earned any money in its life.
Useless and free, it has spent seventy years
as a minor family relic
handed along collaterally to owners
who looked at it sometimes, or didn't bother to.

It must be Nova Scotia; only there
does one see gabled wooden houses
painted that awful shade of brown.
The other houses, the bits that show, are white.
Elm trees, low hills, a thin church steeple
—that gray-blue wisp—or is it? In the foreground
a water meadow with some tiny cows,
two brushstrokes each, but confidently cows;
two miniscule white geese in the blue water,
back-to-back, feeding, and a slanting stick.

Up closer, a wild iris, white and yellow,
fresh-squiggled from the tube.
The air is fresh and cold; cold early spring
clear as gray glass; a half inch of blue sky
below the steel-gray storm clouds.
(They were the artist's specialty.)
A specklike bird is flying to the left.
Or is it a flyspeck looking like a bird?

Heavens, I recognize the place, I know it!
It's behind—I can almost remember the farmer's name.
His barn backed on that meadow. There it is,
titanium white, one dab. The hint of steeple,
filaments of brush-hairs, barely there,
must be the Presbyterian church.
Would that be Miss Gillespie's house?
Those particular geese and cows
are naturally before my time.

A sketch done in an hour, "in one breath,"
once taken from a trunk and handed over.
Would you like this? I'll probably never
have room to hang these things again.
Our Uncle George, no, mine, my Uncle George,
he'd be your great-uncle, left them all with Mother
when he went back to England.
You know, he was quite famous, an R.A. . . .

I never knew him. We both knew this place,
apparently, this literal small backwater,
looked at it long enough to memorize it,
our years apart. How strange. And it's still loved,
or its memory is (it must have changed a lot).
Our visions coincided—"visions" is
too serious a word—our looks, two looks:
art "copying from life" and life itself,
life and the memory of it so compressed

they've turned into each other. Which is which?
Life and the memory of it cramped,
dim, on a piece of Bristol board,
dim, but how live, how touching in detail
—the little that we get for free,
the little of our earthly trust. Not much.
About the size of our abidance
along with theirs: the munching cows,
the iris, crisp and shivering, the water
still standing from spring freshets,
the yet-to-be dismantled elms, the geese.

<hr>

STANLEY PLUMLY ON ELIZABETH BISHOP'S Poem

I think "Poem" is among the very finest of Bishop's *Complete Poems,* often neglected in the anthologies because it seems more "personal" and less "finished" than what this inveterate rewriter is commonly committed to. That's my perception of a perceived misperception. In fact, "Poem" is deeply moving and subtly, richly achieved. It ups the ante on Bishop's quiet habit of making the perfectly finished product look like a poem of process, of worked-out discovery. The epiphanic, elegiac, even philosophic reach of the final stanza pushes the argument—and thus the narrative—well past the keen resonances of her other ode-like poems and evokes a sense of loss equal to that of "One Art" and "Five Flights Up."

"Poem" is one of an odal type that appears throughout Bishop's work, including "Florida," "Over 2000 Illustrations and a Complete Concordance," "At the Fishhouses," and "End of March"—all poems that range between sixty and eighty lines, in lines of eight to twelve syllables, in stanzas that are really verse paragraphs, in forms that open into wider and encompassing speculation. All evince Bishop's impeccable ear and brilliant eye. The "little painting" that represents the ars poetica in "Poem" is anticipated by the much earlier, formally quite different "Large Bad Picture." Although the artist celebrated in each is the same great uncle ("My Uncle George," quoting Bishop's mother), the poems are thirty years apart.

The overall argument of the poem is apparent enough; the intuitive story—and narrative intuition is at the center of Bishop's genius—is less clear. Gut feelings are the basis of her craft, which is why completing a poem took Bishop so much time and territory. The five fluid stanzas of "Poem" develop through presentation, recognition, and realization—or exposition, complication, resolution. It is a dramatic lyric, in other words, as much as it is an analytic lyric. First, the sketch or little painting is rescued, then it is shown to us in painterly detail, then its subject—the entered world of this family relic—is revealed as autobiographic, then its nature is commented on ("a sketch done in an hour"), with a flashback as a footnote, then the connection, or reconciliation, of the two principals—poet and painter, grand-niece and great-uncle—is referenced, thought about, and transformed ("our two visions").

This summary, of course, hardly does justice to what "Poem" is exploring, let alone its language. At different levels of diction, the puns on money versus value, size versus importance, "literal" versus figurative, and life as opposed to (or equal to) memory, suggest some of the terms the poem speaks in. The adverbs are even more sly: the painting has been handed along "collaterally," the cows are "confidently" cows, these particular geese and cows are "naturally" before Bishop's time, and the speaker and the artist both know the place "apparently." The circle of meaning embracing "Poem," from "old-style dollar bill" to, sixty-odd lines later, "the size of our abidance," is powerful in both its specification and its sweep, especially so since the poem interrogates not only the active relationship of art to life but the existential collaboration of the moment and "the memory of it."

"Poem" is a kind of odal elegy—philosophic in its thoughtful impact, moving in its understated, angular conclusion. Rhythmically, the poem builds and builds, with marvelous detail and incredible charm. Then it seems, in its last stanza, to soar before it quickly unwinds, or unbuilds. The size of our abidance, the little that we get for free, is the mortal measure of things here, and that measure applies to our art as it does to our lives, our memory as well as our moment. Bishop's great-uncle's little painting was lost; now it is part of a poem, "in one breath," as the poet puts it. Yeats said that poetry is wasted breath, to which Bishop answers, in "One Art," "(*Write* it!)."

Mirage

R. P. BLACKMUR

The wind was in another country, and
the day had gathered to its heart of noon
the sum of silence, heat, and stricken time.
Not a ripple spread. The sea mirrored
perfectly all the nothing in the sky.
We had to walk about to keep our eyes
from seeing nothing, and our hearts from stopping
at nothing. Then most suddenly we saw
horizon on horizon lifting up
out of the sea's edge a shining mountain
sun-yellow and sea-green; against it surf
flung spray and spume into the miles of sky.
Somebody said mirage, and it was gone,
but there I have been living ever since.

JOHN KOETHE ON R. P. BLACKMUR'S Mirage

"Mirage," by R. P. Blackmur, one of modern poetry's greatest critics, appeared, as best I can ascertain, in his second collection of poems, *The Second World,* published in 1942. It is an unrhymed sonnet, simpler and more direct than much of his poetry, which can be as difficult and cerebral as his criticism. While Blackmur's biographer Russell Fraser is diffident about "Mirage," he describes it as his best-known poem, so it must have attracted a certain amount of attention at one time, although Denis Donoghue does not include it in his 1977 selection of Blackmur's poetry.

I first encountered the poem in a special edition of *The Nassau Lit*—the undergraduate literary magazine at Princeton—devoted to Blackmur and published shortly after his death in 1965. Blackmur was a kind of distant mentor to our coterie of undergraduate poets, who found most other members of the English Department unsympathetic to the poets and poetry that interested us. One of my lasting regrets is that he died just as I was beginning to write poetry in a serious way, so I never met him. But "Mirage" made a deep and lasting impression on me. I find this surprising in retrospect, because my writing at the time, under the influence of Black Mountain poets like Charles Olson and Objectivists like George Oppen, tended to be disjunctive and insistent on the perceived and the concrete, quite unlike the languorous epiphany of the unreal in "Mirage." Yet it may be that my present, somewhat Stevensian way of writing owes something to my encounter with the poem then. It doesn't seem at all dated in the way minor poems from over sixty years ago usually do, and there is a naturalness about it that makes it seem almost contemporary (apart from the slightly stilted feel of the inverted placement of "there" in the last line). The calm and lucid diction, the use of the narrative past tense, and the hallucinatory quality of the images remind me a bit of Mark Strand's poetry—indeed, the mirage of the island even resembles the imagery of some of Strand's recent graphic work, though I have no idea whether there might be any connection between them.

One thing Blackmur was especially attuned to in his critical writing was the way depths of experience can be encapsulated in fleeting nuances of perception, as in these lines he admired from T. S. Eliot's "Dry Salvages": "The salt is on the briar rose / The fog is in the fir trees." It is this mesmerizing power of the barely perceived that is the subject of "Mirage."

I wouldn't want to claim that "Mirage" is a great poem, but I do think it a small marvel. Blackmur was one of our most important and influential critics at a time when poetry enjoyed a stature and central place in culture it no longer possesses. His critical thought is circuitous and intense, but he was also a contrarian and anti-institutionalist; I find the contrast between the intensity of that thought and the transparency of this short blank sonnet enchanting, and in a strange way both unsurprising and exemplary. For that, and for its simple beauty, "Mirage" deserves to be more widely known than it is.

Old Countryside

LOUISE BOGAN

Beyond the hour we counted rain that fell
On the slant shutter, all has come to proof.
The summer thunder, like a wooden bell,
Rang in the storm above the mansard roof,

And mirrors cast the cloudy day along
The attic floor; wind made the clapboards creak.
You braced against the wall to make it strong,
A shell against your cheek.

Long since, we pulled brown oak-leaves to the ground
In a winter of dry trees; we heard the cock
Shout its unplaceable cry, the axe's sound
Delay a moment after the axe's stroke.

Far back, we saw, in the stillest of the year,
The scrawled vine shudder, and the rose-branch show
Red to the thorns, and, sharp as sight can bear,
The thin hound's body arched against the snow.

MARTHA COLLINS ON LOUISE BOGAN'S Old Countryside

Louise Bogan's "Old Countryside" has not been entirely overlooked. In addition to quoting and praising it in his 1961 essay on Bogan, Theodore Roethke seems to have imitated it in his early poem "Interlude" and to have echoed its first line in his later poem "The Tranced" ("We counted several flames in one small fire"). Coincidences, one might think, were it not for his 1959 essay "How to Write Like Somebody Else."

Although I never met her, it was partly by reading Louise Bogan's poems that I learned how to write. She was one of the twentieth century's most careful poets, rarely wasting a word or a metrical substitution—but also one of the most suggestive and deeply psychological. The anthologized poems inevitably reflect the former, but less frequently do full justice to the latter. Although Vincent Engels called it "one of the best poems of 1929" and Harriet Monroe included it in a 1932 anthology, "Old Countryside" has not, to my knowledge, appeared in any recent anthologies.

What first drew me to the poem may have been its exquisite music—or it may have been the fact that I both did and did not know what it was about. The visual and aural images are astonishingly precise and deeply evocative, but they are almost all the poem gives us. The exceptions are the references to time that introduce the summer of the first two stanzas ("Beyond the hour . . . all has come to proof") and the winter of the last two ("Long since"). There is, of course, a "we," suggestive of a relationship of some importance, and it's clear that something has changed besides the seasons; but the poem refuses to say exactly what, instead moving us, as deep memories often do, by image rather than narrative. The fourth stanza, opening with a spondee that parallels the "Long since" of the third, conflates the temporal and spatial and suggests the vividness and process of memory itself: "Far back, we saw, in the stillest of the year."

Throughout, the poem relies equally on the visual and the aural, the latter realized both imagistically and metrically. In the first two stanzas, the noise of rain, thunder, and wind playing on the outside of the house seems mildly menacing, especially in the context of "all has come to proof"; but there is pleasure in both the auditory details themselves and the music that conveys them—the assonance of *shutter / come / summer thunder / above,* for instance, or the stunning metrical substitutions that interrupt the generally smooth iambic meter in an almost celebratory way ("The summer thunder, like a wooden bell, / *Rang in* the storm"). Inside the house, delicate visual images (the mirrors' reflection of clouds, the shell) contrast with the aural impact of the storm outside, but the intimacy and gentle humor of "We counted rain" and "You braced against the wall to make it strong" suggest a comfortable relation to it.

Then, following the silence created by the surprising trimeter line, the poem shifts dramatically. In contrast to the harmonious summer scene, the winter images are random and disturbing; in contrast to the harmonious meter, the music strains the iambic pentameter almost to the breaking point (we almost *hear* "The scrawled vine shudder and rose-branch show / Red to the thorns"). The third stanza repeats the earlier pattern of human activity against a background of external sound, but the enjambment and metrical variations emphasize the disharmony suggested by the fact that the cock's cry is "unplaceable" and (however accurately) the axe's sound delayed. When the last stanza looks beyond the scene into "the stillest of the year," the images become even more emotionally charged: the "scrawled vine" implicitly suggests the human activity of writing, the rose-branch seems to display its red almost consciously, and the hound arching to warm itself resonates with human significance. Without ever saying so, Louise Bogan shows us that the summer thunder indeed had it right, ringing in an emotional storm that is hauntingly realized in the most static and silent images of winter.

Drunken Winter

JOSEPH CERAVOLO

Oak oak! like like
it then
   cold some wild paddle
so sky then;
flea you say
"geese geese" the boy
June of winter
of again
Oak sky

DAVID LEHMAN ON JOSEPH CERAVOLO'S Drunken Winter

Joseph Ceravolo is a great overlooked American poet. Born in the Astoria section of Queens, New York, in 1934, Ceravolo began writing poetry while serving in the U. S. Army in Germany in 1957. He wrote his first poems while on all-night guard duty in a stockade tower. A civil engineer by trade, he studied with Kenneth Koch at the New School in New York City in 1959. Koch's teaching had a strong and lasting influence on him. Frank O'Hara called him "one of the most important poets around," and it was fitting that Ceravolo's debut collection, "Spring in this World of Poor Mutts," won the first Frank O'Hara Award in 1968.

Though little known, Ceravolo's work is admired intensely by those who know it. David Shapiro called Ceravolo "the best religious poet writing in the English language." Asked to name his three favorite poets, Jordan Davis began with Ceravolo then tacked on Whitman and William Carlos Williams. "The Green Lake is Awake," a posthumous volume of Ceravolo's selected poems, won favorable notices in 1994.

Nevertheless, Ceravolo remains a secret ardor in part because the New York School as an entity or category has until perhaps recently eluded academic attention. I love his simplicity—his apparent simplicity, I should say. In reality Ceravolo is, as he writes in his poem "Happiness in the Trees," "no more / simple than a cedar tree / whose children change / the interesting earth / and promise to shake her / before the wind blows / away from you /in the velocity of rest."

Ceravolo uses mostly simple words of few syllables. The effect of their conjunction is startling. He makes the words seem as concrete as objects and as strange. In some instances he resembles a painter who has limited his palette to a few colors used in dazzling combination. In "Drunken Winter," look at how the poem punctuates space. The meaning is in the arrangement. The line breaks, the syntactical breakdown, the spacing, the incidental punctuation (exclamation point, quotation marks) are crucial to our experience of the poem. It's as though a complicated narrative has been reduced to bare essentials delivered breathlessly; what is communicated is not an anecdote but a stammering excitement, charging the words themselves.

In this and other poems, Ceravolo displays an uncanny ability to convey the child's conception of the world. The child seems older in "The Wind Is Blowing West":

> I've been waiting in my tent
> Expecting to go in.
> Have you forgotten to come down?

Can I escape going in?
I was just coming

I was just going in.

Ceravolo pushes the laconic style to achieve a sublime innocence. A six-line poem begins: "O moon / How ghost you are." All the pathos of childhood informs the moment in "Ho Ho Ho Caribou" when the speaker says, "Like a flower, little light, you open / and we make believe / we die."

Ceravolo's poems are lean, full of working nouns and verbs stripped of modifiers. He is unafraid to end a poem abruptly. He can move from whimsy to high tension in a line. Yet none of this finally explains the magic of these poems—how they transform the commonplace into the extraordinary or why they make this reader feel he is in the presence of a natural poet, for whom poems came as freely as leaves to the tree.

Ceravolo lived quietly with his wife and three children in Bloomfield, New Jersey. He was fifty-four when he died of an inoperable tumor on September 4, 1988.

A Trenta-Sei of the Pleasure We Take in the Early Death of Keats

JOHN CIARDI

It is old school custom to pretend to be sad
when we think about the early death of Keats.
The species-truth of the matter is we are glad.
Psilanthropic among exegetes,
I am so moved that when the plate comes by
I almost think to pay the God—but why?

When we think about the early death of Keats
we are glad to be spared the bother of dying ourselves.
His poems are a candy store of bitter-sweets.
We munch whole flights of angels from his shelves
drooling a sticky glut, almost enough
to sicken us. But what delicious stuff!

The species-truth of the matter is we are glad
to have a death to munch on. Truth to tell,
we are also glad to pretend it makes us sad.
When it comes to dying, Keats did it so well
we thrill to the performance. Safely here,
this side of the fallen curtain, we stand and cheer.

Psilanthropic among exegetes,
as once in a miles-high turret spitting flame,
I watched boys flower through orange winding sheets
and shammed a mourning because it put a name
to a death I might have taken—which in a way
made me immortal for another day

I was so moved that when the plate came by
I had my dollar in hand to give to death
but changed to a penny—enough for the old guy,
and almost enough saved to sweeten my breath
with a toast I will pledge to the Ape of the Divine
in thanks for every death that spares me mine.

I almost thought of paying the God—but why?
Had the boy lived, he might have grown as dull
as Tennyson. Far better, I say, to die
and leave us a formed feeling. O beautiful,
pale, dying poet, fading as soft as rhyme,
the saddest music keeps the sweetest time.

John Ciardi devised the form of the trenta-sei (thirty-six, in Italian) in 1985. It had its first publication after his death in the 1989 volume *Echoes: Poems Left Behind.* One wouldn't expect the form to have worked its way into the consciousness of many poets by now, but it's somewhat surprising to me that three or four haven't been sufficiently intrigued to accept the challenge and explore the possibilities it presents.

This certainly is not the first time a poet has turned from the path of tradition and invented a form. In a number of such instances, the new way of going has found fertile ground in the minds of poets around the world. Not long after Petrarch invented the sonnet in the fourteenth century, poets in several languages were making good use of it. Spenser's modification of the form some 200 years later carried his name and inclination around the planet, as did Shakespeare's variation a few years later. Franco Bernini's caudate sonnet—the tail was tacked on about 1500—didn't stir nearly as much interest, but a lot of them have been written, and they're still taking shape. Arnaut Daniel turned his hand around 1200 to the invention of the sestina. Jean Passerat devised the villanelle around 1570. In 1989, John Ciardi gave us the trenta-sei.

The poem consists of six six-line stanzas rhyming *ababcc*, with lines two through six in stanza one becoming line one of a following stanza, in that order. As a resolving device, he allows the fifth line of stanza one to change from the present tense to the past when it appears as the first line of stanza five.

As in other works by John Ciardi, the line is clearly the unit of the poem, a unit at the same time of sound, sense, and syntax, so that the reader progressing through the poem feels solid ground underfoot. At the same time, most of the lines raise a question, in the mind of the reader, that the next line will answer:

> The species-truth of the matter is we are glad *(of what?)*
> to have a death to munch on. Truth to tell, *(which truth is what?)*
> we are also glad to pretend it makes us sad.
> When it comes to dying, Keats did it so well *(how well?)*
> we thrill to the performance . . .

And so forth, building for the reader a compelling sense of forward motion.

Ciardi's rarest accomplishment in this poem, apart from the prosodic form, is the closing of a thought with the closing of each stanza. It's not often that we find a poet so clearly in control of the poem.

The resolution of the poem is perhaps its finest moment: It looks back on itself and says to the reader—inductively, so that she can take it home—"This is what the poem is getting at," and says it with such finality that if it were the last line on the page, one would not turn the page to see if the poem ended there. The poem doesn't just end: it resolves.

All of this is to say that John Ciardi has done what the maker of any artwork wants to do, which is to make the very difficult look easy, to give form to the wildest feelings, and—though this rarely happens—to give the art a shape it didn't have before. One would think that such a shape in poetry would begin to appear in anthologies and textbooks, and that other poets would be persuaded by the intriguing challenges and possibilities to write their own trenta-seis.

Whatever Happened to Don Ho

TOM CLARK

I used to watch Hawaii Five Oh
in Bolinas
but not on television
it used to cross
the northwestern sky
in yellow thunder strikes
making tiger violets
stripe the early nights
which were so wet and deep
you could love and live and
let live in your little GTO
and I could drift out back

and drop my sleepy sack
amid the plants
and play "easy street"
on the 12 string
I never thought your flesh wd wither
whether or not
history came to pass and I never
thought we wd enter Time
I had a good reason
for taking the easy
day trip into skyfulness
night after night
it took me so long to find out
but I found out
so here I am lost in the present again
forgotten but not gone
with an imaginary ukulele on my knee
and a wide grin only in my
don ho imitation I dont do for you anymore

BILLY COLLINS ON TOM CLARK'S Whatever Happened to Don Ho

Considering how easily the majority of people manage to overlook the very existence of poetry, one could probably locate a poem that deserved more attention by simply throwing a dart blindfolded at the wall of American poetry.

But let us lay that complaint aside and zero in. If that same wall were to be papered over with poems by Tom Clark, I could throw the dart blindfolded and, odds are, hit one I really liked.

Let's say the dart happened to land on "Whatever Happened to Don Ho," one of my favorites though it does not appear in my favorite Tom Clark book, *John's Heart.* I bought that book in 1972 at LaGuardia airport according to a notation on the inside cover. I remember being intrigued by the presence of a new hardbound book by a hip West Coast poet among the usual crime and romance airport-reads. My dog was so impressed by the book, he almost ate it after I got it home. So

John's Heart is my favorite because its chewed-up cover reminds me of 1972—an exciting year for the young at heart—and of the dog, a golden retriever named Luke who was run over a couple of years later on the road outside the house I was renting.

But back to the poem with the dart in it, "Whatever Happened to Don Ho." Like so many Tom Clark poems, this one dares to be deceptively loose, so druggy, and so American, or should I say Hawaiian. The Bolinas of the poem, as you may know, is a small, secluded northern California town which was a haven for poetry, psychedelics, and other creative activities in the late '60s and '70s, a place so protected from outsiders that the locals would routinely remove any road signs that pointed the way to their flowery enclave as fast as the highway department could pound them in. It was there that television programs could be viewed in the sky and catchphrases from Beach Boys' songs perfumed the air.

That dart seemed to know what it was doing because the Don Ho poem typifies so many beguiling aspects of Clark's style. The poem glides through itself with Clark's usual and enviable ease, and not just because of the absence of punctuation, though that's worth noting. "Money is strange on LSD," another Bolinas resident observed, and so is punctuation, it might be added. I know of no poet, with the stunning exception of Merwin, who has gotten along so well—achieved such liberation, really—without the etiquette of the comma and period, not to mention the semicolon, "the valet of phraseology," in Nicholson Baker's words.

The poem moves on the oiled surface of a stoned—but crafty—consciousness, and we witness the poet in the act of trusting his own associations as they occur. The result is a light, flexible, playful display of movement. But as usual, something is rumbling beneath the playground. Here, we might notice the quiet shift in the poem's middle from the goofy to the profound as the poem descends to touch on lyric poetry's oldest theme, mortality—a shift signaled by the near Shakespearean "your flesh wd wither." If you are inclined to look at a poem as a series of maneuvers, this would be a good one to study.

The poem finds its destination in the comic-melancholy self-portrait of the artist as a player of the air-ukulele, now sadly past fooling around with the withered, Time-bound, and presumably romantic "you." But not before the paradoxical play of "lost in the present" and the sweet reversal of the "forgotten but not gone."

Ever since I first found a few of his poems tucked into the back pages of *Rolling Stone,* Tom Clark has been a model for me. He is one of the strong poets who has managed to restore wit to its original place in poetry. And his voice has spread its sense of cool and its feeling for the ridiculous from the late '60s right into the very foyer of the twenty-first century with its potted plants and scary-looking doorman.

Let's end with another throw of the dart which this time happens to land on a tiny Clark number titled "Fucked Mind."

> Then we see 3 raccoons by the door.
> They're wearing visors.
> They're exactly Jessica's size.
>
> They're very out front.
> It's all I can do to get behind them.

Anybody else want a throw?

from Like the Molave

R. ZULUETA DA COSTA

My American friend continues:
> you are a nation being played for a sucker;
> you are susceptible to lachrymal inducement:
> a man comes to you with a sobtale and soon
> you are a poorfish swallowing hook-line-and-sinker.

And I answer with parable of analogy:
> one adventured into port and called brothers;
> we fed him with the milk and honey of the land;
> he filled his pockets by the sweat of the little brown
> brother and packed for home,
> taking with him but one song for souvenir:
> the monkeys have no tails in Zamboanga.

The lady visitor wishes to study Filipino culture and life:
  our museums are open, our history rich with generations;
  under her nose at every turn the vital life of a child-nation,
  beating its hopeful beat with eager avian pulse;
  giving her tokens: a mestiza dress, a bamboo flute, a song.
  she gives something in return: she pays an urchin to undress
  and pose climbing a coconut tree for the folks back home.

  Over and over returning parable.
  Friend, are these the ways of the West?
  Friend, this is not the American way.

The little brown brother opens his eyes to the glorious sound of
  the Star Spangled;
  dreams to the grand tune of the American dream;
  is proud to be part of the sweeping American magnitude;
  strains his neck upon the rising skyscraper of American ideals,
  and on it hinges faith, hope, aspiration;
  sings the American epic of souls conceived in liberty;
  quivers with longing brotherhood of men created equal;
  envisions great visions of the land across the sea where dwell
  his strong brothers.

And then the fact. The crushing fact of a world no longer shining
  through the exalted word;
  the world where is the deed, the intolerable deed.

Across the sea the little brown brother is no longer a creature
    terrorized by hatred, shamed by contempt and the sting of
    prejudice:
  he is a child fondling the smashed remains of a toy given by
  mother and by mother shattered;
  he is a child wondering, questioning, are these the ways of a
    mother?
  he is a child perplexed and hurt, yet fondling the ghost of a toy;
  hoping and hoping mother will mend the toy.

The repatriate returns sullen and broken: he is that child. We know
   the story, the black looks, the scowls, the placards in the
   restaurants saying: *Neither Dogs nor Filipinos Allowed;* the
   warning at the fair: *Beware of Filipino Pickpockets;* the loneliness,
   the woman denied.

Yet, what say you, repatriate? America is a great land.
Dear child, hoping and hoping mother will mend the toy.

The emigrant thinks: surely if we welcome the big white brother
   blasting the gold out of our hills, surely, the little brown
   brother will not be begrudged the picking of lettuce leaves from
      his fields.
Dear child, hoping and hoping.

The Shanghai refugee arrives: this is the new home.
The Jewish refugee arrives: this is the new home.
The Hongkong refugee arrives: this is the new home.

   Philippines, you are not a sucker.
   Philippines, you are the molave child, questioning, wondering,
      perplexed, hurt;
      the molave child hoping and hoping mother will mend
      the shattered toy.

NICK CARBÓ ON R. ZULUETA DA COSTA'S Like the Molave

Rafael Zulueta da Costa's long poem, "Like the Molave," is one of
the most important touchstones in the history of Philippine poetry in
English. The book, *Like the Molave & Other Poems,* was the top prize-
winner in poetry in the 1940 Commonwealth Literary Contest. When
one considers the history of America's colonial domination of the Phil-
ippine archipelago since 1898, its imposition of American culture and
language, and repression of native cultural expression, this set of liter-
ary prizes was the beginning of the official recognition of local writers.
When the American forces sent by President McKinley arrived on the

shores of Manila Bay in 1898, few Americans back home knew where the Philippine islands were on a map. Cartoon images of Filipino "savages," portraying the locals as "Negroes" with big lips and bones adorning their heads, filled the American newspapers of the day. Rudyard Kipling had written his famous poem "White Man's Burden" to exhort the Americans to earn their place in the sun by accepting the charge of these "brown pickaninnies" and by civilizing them. By 1940, the Filipinos had been educated by the Americans for more than four decades and a new generation of English-speaking writers was about to come to the fore. The first anthology of Filipino-English verse appeared a mere sixteen years earlier. The editor of *Filipino Poetry*, Rodolfo Dato, wrote in his introduction an apologia for the existence of the book and quoted the American educator and linguist Frank C. Laubach on the literary ability of the Filipinos:

> They [the Filipinos] knew nothing of the English language prior to the American occupation. Their attempts at composing prose and poetry in English have been so full of grammatical errors and mis-use of words, that Americans have not been in any mood to look for dreams to which the Filipinos have been struggling to give utterance.

By 1940, the dreams of Filipino poets writing in English were reaching a maturity which the Americans could no longer ignore. "Like the Molave" begins with the invocation of the Filipino national hero José Rizal, who was executed by the Spanish colonial government in 1896: "Not yet, Rizal, not yet. Sleep not in peace." Da Costa calls to Rizal's spirit and implores him to rise from the ashes of history to attend to the current struggle against a new colonial master:

> Our shoulders are not strong; our sinews are
> Grown flaccid with dependence, smug with ease
> Under another's wing. Rest not in peace;
> Not yet, Rizal, not yet . . .

The main reason that the judges cited the book as worthy of the prize was the poem's political content. In the introduction to "Like the Molave," the Filipino critic Salvador P. Lopez says: "Here is poetry that is as large in its social sympathies as the sweep of its resonant lines is large; poetry that is exultant because it exalts the common man. Rarely has the Social Muse been courted in language of surer accent and more irresistible persuasion. . . ." These social sympathies that won Zulueta da Costa wide literary acclaim in certain literary circles also got him into trouble with many American officials who interpreted some of the lines in "Like the Molave" as blatantly anti-American. Lines like "We know / the story, the black looks, the scowls, the placards in the / restaurants saying: *Neither Dogs nor Filipinos allowed;* the / warning at the fair: *Beware of Filipino pickpockets;* the loneliness, / the woman denied" and "The emigrant thinks: surely if we welcome the big white brother / blasting the gold out of our hills, surely, the little brown / brother will not be begrudged the picking of lettuce leaves from his fields." cost the winning poet his teaching job at the De LaSalle College. When he presented his résumé at newspaper offices and private businesses in Manila, no one would give him a job.

The story of "Like the Molave" in Philippine cultural history took an upbeat turn during the '50s, '60s, and '70s when the poem was made required reading in every high school classroom from the islands of Luzon to Mindanao. The poet, however, did not publish another book of poems during the rest of his life because of the deep glorious wounds received when he dared to stand up against the American imperialist gale.

[This World is not Conclusion]

EMILY DICKINSON

This World is not Conclusion.
A Species stands beyond—
Invisible, as Music—
But positive, as Sound—
It beckons, and it baffles—
Philosophy—don't know—
And through a Riddle, at the last—
Sagacity must go—
To guess it, puzzles scholars—

To gain it, Men have borne
Contempt of Generations
And Crucifixion, shown—
Faith slips—and laughs, and rallies—
Blushes, if any see—
Plucks at a twig of Evidence—
And asks a Vane, the way—
Much gesture, from the Pulpit—
Strong Hallelujahs roll—
Narcotics cannot still the Tooth
That nibbles at the soul—

RICHARD FOERSTER ON EMILY DICKINSON'S
[This World is not Conclusion]

In 1992, after reading Judith Farr's fine critical biography *The Passion of Emily Dickinson,* in which she explores Dickinson's "honorable and courageous skepticism about Christian dogma" and her lifelong wrestlings with the big themes of death, immortality, and the nature of God, I felt compelled for the first time to read *The Complete Poems* in its entirety. The "Greatest Hits" of the anthologists, I quickly discovered, barely hinted at the breadth of Dickinson's accomplishment. I found myself moving with delight through the largely uncharted territory of Thomas H. Johnson's edition. About a third of the way, I encountered #501—"This World is not Conclusion"—and was immediately beckoned and baffled by the poem's seemingly easy affirmation of an afterlife. The poem, however, would certainly have been a failure without the twist that Dickinson adds after line twelve: "Faith slips," she writes, and in the ensuing images we can see that she is developing a personification—of someone stumbling and trying to regain her composure with awkward, yet good-humored self-awareness. As Faith continues on her uncertain way, she asks a weathervane for guidance and proceeds past pulpit and congregation, immune to the narcotics of organized religion that would "still the Tooth / That nibbles at the soul—" (Could Dickinson, writing in 1862, have encountered Marx's earlier metaphor equating religion with opium?) I love that closing image of God's presence as some kind of spiritual toothache. Or is it fear of Death that nibbles at the soul—a fear which religion cannot still? Like all good poems, this one maintains a certain mystery and the possibility of alternate readings.

Dickinson's biographers, as far as I know, include no discussion of this poem. Perhaps they think it a minor effort or so transparent as to need no gloss, but I find myself returning to this poem time and again. It speaks to me on a personal level, as a spiritual being wrestling with my own feelings about religious dogma and the ineffable nature of God. It also speaks to me on a broader social level. While rereading the poem during the writing of this essay, my mind kept settling uneasily on the Islamic suicide bombers' unswerving certainty in a merited afterlife and on the radical zealotry of the perpetrators of the September 11 terror. Dickinson challenges such obsessions and tempers them with humble doubt. I was amused to discover that when this poem first appeared in 1896, after the poet's death, her editors censored the last eight lines, no doubt to protect her from being judged an inadequate Christian—no doubt failing to see the salutary wisdom of letting Faith slip and fall on its face from time to time, then letting it rally on its own, guided by natural instincts.

Out of her lifelong questioning and grappling, out of the tension she created between acceptance on the one hand and denial on the other—what I call Emily Dickinson's passionate uncertainty—came a great flowering of poetry: 1,775 sharp, concise, idiosyncratic, rebellious, probing poems, like this overlooked gem, that stand as a testament to a uniquely American voice which claims to represent the deep concerns of us all. Dickinson's poetry is never a palliative for our souls but rather a tonic that offers us the strength to wrestle with life's mysteries. She gives voice to that invisible music just beyond our senses and does so without the accompaniment of rolling Hallelujahs or the dogmatist's Gesture. The wind of truth behind her words points, like her weathervane, in no single, unswerving direction. This poem, like so many others of hers, propels us toward a middle ground of the imagination, somewhere beyond doubt but far from certainty. Her poetry pins any fanatical rant to the mat.

[A Pit—but Heaven over it—]

EMILY DICKINSON

A Pit—but Heaven over it—
And Heaven beside, and Heaven abroad,
and yet a Pit—
With Heaven over it.

To stir would be to slip—
To look would be to drop—
To dream—to sap the Prop
That holds my chances up.
Ah! Pit! With Heaven over it!

The depth is all my thought—
I dare not ask my feet—
'Twould start us where we sit
So straight you'd scarce suspect
It was a Pit—with fathoms under it—
Its Circuit just the same.
Seed-summer-tomb—
Whose Doom to whom?

RAE ARMANTROUT ON EMILY DICKINSON'S
[A Pit—but Heaven over it—]

Emily Dickinson is certainly not an overlooked poet, but she was very prolific, and many of her poems are seldom read. When I was preparing a presentation on Dickinson for the 1999 Modernism conference, I came upon a striking poem I'd never read before. It's numbered 1712 by Johnson and 508 by Franklin. (I am using the Johnson version.) The date of composition is uncertain, but it was first published in *Bolts of Melody* (1945), edited by Mabel Todd. No autograph copy of the poem now exists. This raises the theoretical question of whether it is genuine. To me it seems likely enough that it is. Who but Dickinson could have been so intense, so peculiar, so bold?

As everyone knows, Dickinson was obsessed with mortality and questions of faith. This poem puts those concerns in relentless conjunction/collision. The reader is sent in a dizzying "Circuit," or oscillation, between "Pit" and "Heaven." Dickinson uses the word "pit" four times and "heaven" five, yet "pit" predominates: It is the only one of the pair to make it into the third stanza. We need to stop and imagine this pit. Is it hell or is it the grave? In other words, is it theological or physical? Is Heaven where God reigns, or is it the sky above and around the earth? The poem, at least as I see it, oscillates violently between these readings. The poem begins with what sounds like a conventional message of consolation, Christianity's response to death or evil. There is "A Pit—but Heaven over it—/And Heaven beside and Heaven abroad," but the third line pivots hard away from consolation: "And yet a Pit—." The "but" of the first line is reversed with a telling "yet."

In the second stanza, the speaker is immobilized over the Pit—or is she already in her grave? She can't stir, she can't look, she can't even dream. She can only wait, a still point of blank concentration. "To dream—to sap the Prop/that holds my chances up." Those are some of the most mysterious and interesting lines in the poem. What is this "Prop?" It sounds almost comically material and artificial, a lever to hoist the speaker's hopes above the pit of despair. Flimsy as a theatrical prop, it is threatened with collapse. (What would Lacan say?)

Beginning in the third stanza, her attention is drawn downward: "The depth is all my thought—," "It was a Pit—with fathoms under it—." Lines like this make me shiver. Now an abyss opens *below* the Pit to match the heaven above, "Its Circuit just the same." The poem ends with a tolling boom of sound-alike words: "Whose Doom to whom?" Identity becomes irrelevant here, lost among circulating echoes.

The surface of this poem is more troubled and schizoid than most of Dickinson's work. The poem is also grotesque and comic: We (the first person becomes plural in the last stanza) are frightened into practicing good posture (". . . where we sit / So straight you'd scarce suspect / It was a Pit . . .") in or just over an abyss.

Gilligan's Island

TIM DLUGOS

The Professor and Ginger are standing in the space in front
of the Skipper's cabin. The Professor is wearing deck shoes,
brushed denim jeans, and a white shirt open at the throat.
Ginger is wearing spike heels, false eyelashes, and a white
satin kimono. The Professor looks at her with veiled lust
in his eyes. He raises an articulate eyebrow and addressees
her as Cio-Cio-San. Ginger blanches and falls on her knife.

· · · · ·

Meanwhile it is raining in northern California. In a tiny
village on the coast, Rod Taylor and Tippi Hedren are totally
concerned. They realize that something terrible is happening.
Each has been savagely attacked by a wild songbird within
the last twenty-four hours. Outside their window thousands
of birds have gathered in anticipation of the famous school-
yard scene. Tippi Hedren is wearing a colorful lipstick.

· · · · ·

Ginger stares back at the Professor. His sullen good looks
are the perfect foil for her radiant smile. The Skipper and
Gilligan come into sight. The Skipper has been chasing
Gilligan around the lagoon for a long time now. Gilligan
holds onto his hat in the stupid way he has of doing things
like that. The Professor's lips part in a sneer of perfect
contempt. Ginger bares her teeth, as if in appreciation.

· · · · ·

Jackie Kennedy bares her teeth. Behind and above her, the
muzzle of a high-powered rifle protrudes from a window. A little
man is aiming at Jackie Kennedy's husband. The man is wearing
bluejeans and a white T-shirt. There isn't a bird to be seen.
As he squeezes the trigger, the little man mutters between
clenched teeth, "Certs is a candy mint." The hands of Jackie
Kennedy's husband jerk automatically toward his head.

The Professor is noticing Ginger's breasts. He thinks of
the wife he left at home, who probably thinks he's dead.
He thinks of his mother, and all of the women he has ever
known. Mr. and Mrs. Howell are asleep in their hut, secure
in their little lives as character actors. Ginger shifts her
weight to the other foot. The intensity of the moment reminds
the Professor of a Japanese city before the end of the war.

· · · · ·

In his mind he goes down each aisle in his government class,
focusing on each face, each body. He is lying on his bed
with his white shirt off and his trousers open. Dorothy
Kirsten's voice fills the room. He settles on a boy who sits
two desks behind him. He begins to masturbate, his body moving
in time with the sad music. At moments like these he feels
farthest away. As he shoots, his lips part and he bares his teeth.

· · · · ·

The Professor and Ginger are watching each other across the
narrow space. The Skipper and Gilligan have disappeared down
the beach. The Howells are quietly snoring. The Professor
and Ginger are alone. From the woods comes the sound of
strange birds. From the water comes a thick and eerie
tropical silence. The famous conversation scene is about
to start. Clouds appear in the sky, and it begins to snow.

DAVID TRINIDAD ON TIM DLUGOS' Gilligan's Island

Tim Dlugos wrote "Gilligan's Island" in the mid-'70s, a time when
old TV shows were only available in reruns and old films only on the
late show or at the local art theater. John F. Kennedy's assassination
was still felt as a collective trauma, something we could still remember
experiencing, rather than a conspiracy; it had yet to become a movie.
In those pre-VCR/Nick at Nite days, there was a sense that the sitcoms

and motion pictures many of us had grown up watching would gradually fade to black as we took our roles as adults in an adult society. Dlugos' poem turned such a presumption on its ear. Those silly characters and inane plots are *in* us, the poem announced. Those flickering images are more indelible than anyone would have thought; they aren't ever going to go away. Dlugos was there, just ahead of the curve, to tell us that.

The poem is deceptively entertaining, a definite crowd pleaser, and yet its complexities, its disturbing implications, are immediate. The internalization of actual and artificial horror, the marketing of JFK's death (prescient here), the loneliness and isolation of the boy "playing back" the image of another student as he masturbates. Everything—movies, history, objects of desire—viewed from the same impassive distance. And everything interfused. TV screens, movie screens, the "screen" of reality, reality seen on a TV screen, the screen of our own imaginations: we are all stuck in the same whirlpool of stock images. A society of voyeurs—insulated from experience, numb to actual touch. We are all stranded on *Gilligan's Island*.

Tim Dlugos was born in 1950 and grew up in Arlington, Virginia. As a young adult, he lived in Philadelphia and Washington, D.C., before moving to New York City in 1976. There he became a prominent poet in the downtown literary scene. His association with Dennis Cooper in Los Angeles in the early '80s led to an exciting cross-country camaraderie among younger poets: Amy Gerstler, Jack Skelley, Elaine Equi, Jerome Sala, Eileen Myles, and Brad Gooch, to name just a few. Dlugos died of AIDS in 1990, when he was forty. I was lucky enough to have been touched, personally, by Tim's effervescent genius, and to have edited his selected poems, *Powerless,* in 1996. Sad truth: Dlugos' entire body of work—over 500 poems—is overlooked, especially the amazing and moving poems he wrote as he was dying of AIDS. Dennis Cooper has written: "If not for the peculiar shape of the poetry world, Tim Dlugos would be major." I've always believed that the finest work rises, sooner or later, to the surface, receives the recognition it deserves. I'm still holding out hope that Tim's eventually will.

[Show me, dear Christ, Thy spouse, so bright and clear]

JOHN DONNE

Show me, dear Christ, Thy spouse, so bright and clear.
What! Is it She, which on the other shore
Goes richly painted? or which robb'd and tore
Laments and mourns in Germany and here?
Sleeps she a thousand, then peeps up one year?
Is she self truth and errs? Now new, now outwore?
Doth she, and did she, and shall she evermore
On one, on seven, or on no hill appear?
Dwells she with us, or like adventuring knights
First travel we to seek and then make love?
Betray kind husband Thy spouse to our sights,
And let mine amorous soul court Thy mild dove,
Who is most true, and pleasing to Thee, then
When she is embrac'd and open to most men.

PAUL MULDOON ON JOHN DONNE'S [Show me, dear Christ,
Thy spouse, so bright and clear]

John Donne (1572–1631) wrote some of the most provocative poems
in the English language, a category into which "Show me, dear Christ
. . ." would certainly fit. Its provocation is based, as is generally the case
with Donne, on the far-fetched nature of the conceit at its heart, a con-
ceit being the extended metaphor involving "heterogeneous ideas yoked
by violence together" for which Doctor Johnson scolded the Metaphys-
ical poets in general and Donne in particular.

The outlandish metaphor here is twofold. One aspect involves a
comparative commonplace, that of the church equaling the bride of
Christ, an idea that is an extension of the comparison of the church to
the "body" of Christ in Ephesians 1:22–23. The other aspect involves
another commonplace, that the Catholic Church is a "whore," an idea
drawing on the relationship between the Whore of Babylon and Rome,

which is sometimes substantiated by the image in Revelations 17:9 of the Whore sitting on "seven hills," an image picked up in lines seven and eight of the poem:

> Doth she, and did she, and shall she evermore
> On one, on seven, or on no hill appear.

The combination of these two commonplace ideas of "bride" and "whore" leads to the startling freshness of the final paradox of the poem, whereby the church "bride" is "most true" to the Christ "groom":

> When she is embrac'd and open to most men.

The first sense in which this poem might be described as overlooked has to do with the sense of inevitability of this resolution, which strikes us with the justice of an idea that we imagine we've somehow always known but upon which we've somehow only happened. There's something shocking about the fact that the resolution is indeed "most true and pleasing," if only for the duration of the poem.

That the poem has any duration, in the sense of its having lasted, is almost as tenuous a matter. To begin with, almost none of Donne's poetry was published during his lifetime. After his death, and certainly throughout most of the 17th and 18th centuries, he was barely read. It was only with editions by James Russell Lowell in 1895 and E. K. Chambers in 1896 that his poetry was, in any general sense, rediscovered. This poem had to wait until 1899, and Edmund Gosse's edition of *The Life and Letters of John Donne,* to see the light of day.

Despite the fact that I've been reading John Donne in a way that I might once have described as "religiously" (Donne was, of course, a Catholic who became the Protestant Dean of St. Paul's, so the hair-splitting subject matter of the poem would have had a particular resonance for him), I had somehow managed to miss this poem. It may be that I was reeling from the effect of so many of the other "Holy Sonnets," including the attention-grabbing "Batter my heart, three-person'd God," "Spit in my face you Jews," "Death be not proud," and "At the round earth's imagin'd corners," and I wasn't physically fit to read it. That's why I now overlook the others and begin with "Show me, dear Christ."

True Night

ALVIN FEINMAN

So it is midnight, and all
The angels of ordinary day gone,
The abiding absence between day and day
Come like true and only rain
Comes instant, eternal, again:

As though an air had opened without sound
In which all things are sanctified,
In which they are at prayer—
The drunken man in his stupor,
The madman's lucid shrinking circle;

As though all things shone perfectly,
Perfected in self-discrepancy:
The widow wedded to her grief,
The hangman haloed in remorse—
I should not rearrange a leaf,

No more than wish to lighten stones
Or still the sea where it still roars—
Here every grief requires its grief,
Here every longing thing is lit
Like darkness at an altar.

As long as truest night is long,
Let no discordant wing
Corrupt these sorrows into song.

REGINALD SHEPHERD ON ALVIN FEINMAN'S True Night

One of the most talented and underappreciated poets of his generation, Alvin Feinman was born in 1929 and raised in New York City. Although always committed to poetry ("even doggerel narratives in early childhood," he says), he had originally decided on philosophy as a career and did graduate work at Yale to that end, until he realized that the dominant analytical school excluded all the important philosophical questions. It was in poetry that those unanswerable questions—of knowledge, perception, and the relation between being and appearance—could properly be addressed. As Feinman has somewhat jocularly said, "I was, even philosophically, convinced that, as I liked to put it, if according to Aristotle, 'Poetry is more philosophical than history,' so is it more philosophical than philosophy. The work I'd have had to do in philosophy would be to lay out the grounds for privileging poetry—which indeed our era has been more or less doing—via Heidegger, Rorty, Derrida, etc."

Although he has been listed by Harold Bloom as part of the essential canon of Western literature, and Bloom has written that "the best of his poems stand with the most achieved work of his generation, with the best of Ashbery, Merrill, Ammons, Hollander, and only a few others," Feinman's work has only been anthologized six times (in volumes published in the late 1960s and early '70s, most now out of print). He is not included in any of the "canonical" anthologies of modern or modern American poetry, not even one such as Cary Nelson's recent Oxford anthology, which explicitly aims to recover and rediscover neglected writers. Nor is Feinman listed in the purportedly comprehensive *Contemporary Authors*. His first book, *Preambles and Other Poems,* was published by Oxford University Press in 1965, to much praise from such figures as Allen Tate, Conrad Aiken, Geoffrey Hartman, and Bloom. Now out of print, it was reissued with a handful of additional poems by Princeton University Press as *Poems* in 1990; that volume is also out of print. In part, Feinman's lack of a wide reputation and audience is due to the unabashed difficulty of his work, which disdains the easy consolations of autobiography or narrative. In larger measure, this neglect is perhaps due to his own eschewing of the literary world's elevation of the trivia of publicity and competition over the pursuit of serious aesthetic accomplishment.

Alvin Feinman is a true visionary poet, heir to Stevens and Crane in the modern line and, further back, to Blake, Wordsworth, and Shelley: poets who invented human consciousness as a subject for poetry. His poems demand much of the reader (at times resisting the intelligence almost successfully, as Stevens said a poem should), but they offer many rewards in return, not least those of dazzling imagery (light and the work light does is omnipresent in his work) and dense, rich music. Like much of the best poetry, it can be enjoyed before it is understood.

John Hollander has written that Feinman's poetry explores the boundary between the visible and the visionary. In one of the blurbs for *Preambles,* Conrad Aiken wrote that Feinman's work was "true metaphysical poetry," and Feinman's philosophical background is evident in his work. The poems constitute an epistemological and phenomenological investigation of the world, a probing of the surfaces of things that moves from seeing to seeing-into to seeing-through to the other side of appearances, the luminous interior of the material world. As Bloom has written, the "opposition between the imaginative self and reality seems as central to these poems as it was to Stevens' and as grandly articulated."

"True Night" is a lovely example of what Bloom calls "a central sensibility seeking imaginative truth without resorting to any of the available evasions of consciousness," whose temptations are both acknowledged and refused. The poem opens at midnight, "The abiding absence between day and day," a present absence which is both instant (and *an* instant) and eternal, because it is no given day and no single time, but rather the moment between dates. This no-time is all times, both everlasting and utterly ephemeral. It is (or rather, it is "As though"—what we know is not the thing itself, but only its appearance, our own knowing of it) an air that has opened soundlessly, that we take into ourselves with every breath. Particularly within the precincts of a poem, the phrase "an air," in conjunction with the evocation of sound, calls up a pun on the Renaissance sense of an "air" as a song. Here, it is a song without sound; Keats wrote that unheard melodies are sweetest, and this soundless air is sweeter than any song one could ever hear.

Here in this time, which is no time, the polarity of identity and difference is suspended, and opposites meet. Things are beside themselves, at peace with their own restlessness and discontent, their own failure to be identical with themselves: they are "Perfected in self-discrepancy," like the off-rhyme of the words "perfectly" and "discrepancy." All wrongs are posed in the perfection of a still life, no less wrong but now transfigured into necessity and equipoise: "Here every grief requires its grief." The poet's task is both to capture this momentless moment and to leave it undisturbed, to turn its untouchability into art without marring or altering it. The line "I should not rearrange a leaf" can be read either as "I wouldn't rearrange a leaf even if I could, all is perfect as it is" or as "I should abandon any desire to rearrange a leaf, to insert my own will into the seen/scene." For this poem, paradise is paradox, where longing (the source of suffering, according to the Buddha) is illumination, and to be lit is to be like darkness "at an altar," at prayer, prayed to, or both.

The poem's last stanza insists that no discordant wing (shattering the harmony of the soundless air) should be allowed to corrupt the sorrows the poem presents into song, at least "As long as truest night is long." That is to say, this admonition holds both forever and only for the most fleeting of (non-)moments. And yet the poem itself, unavoidably, is a song ("lyric," after all, comes from "lyre"), voiced and heard. The poem both "mystically" asserts a paradoxical concord (echoing and amplifying Stevens' avowal that "The imperfect is our paradise") and takes a potentially ironic stance toward it: the poem is both entranced and undeluded.

The inescapable paradox of "True Night," the truth that it both embodies and struggles against in the name of truth, is that the poem's discordant wing *has* corrupted the scene into song: it is helpless not to do so, for otherwise there would be no poem. But the poem has also acknowledged and honored the difference between scene and song: it has reminded us that *is* remains *is* however much mind and music might wish it otherwise, however much metaphor and song might wish to translate being into seeming.

Dark Old Men

PENNY GASAWAY

i love dark old men: men born in cotton patches raised on
white folk's leavings—mothers off cooking cleaning singing
lullabies to chalk-toned children. men who carried salt-pork
hoe cakes and ribbon cane syrup in rex lard buckets
to the fields or school for supper.
men who remember the poll tax and think poll means penis
who bought black pussy for a dime and know what the blue balls are.
i love dark old men nurtured by jim crow who sat at the back of the bus
knocked on closed doors and waited at the colored entrance for a
seat in the segregated dark of a third floor balcony.
old men who stepped into the street as a white woman passed
who tipped their hats lowered brown eyes and voices said "yes ma'am"
and "yes sir" even to—especially to—white trash.
i love dark old men who escaped west from mississippi louisiana
arkansas and texas. men hired by southern pacific to build a
railroad—who signed a contract and caught a train to avoid
a chain who marched from union station straight down central
avenue popped a rag and opened a shine parlor. chauffeurs who
answered extra calls moonlighting as indians. single men
who lived in service up third story stairs existing alone
beneath bel-air roofs in attic rooms saving . . .
every other thursday and sundays off.
i love dark old men who fathered children
on ladies who drove them out after the act
enrolling on relief—father unknown.
i love old men who have been called boy all their lives.
i love dark old men who take you to motel rooms
filled with mirrors and with callused hands
undress you slowly pulling you
apart layer by layer and when you stand naked
run their slow eyes over your body.
men who take you into blue tiled showers
cover you with thick scented lather
cup your tits with soapy black hands and run

slippery fingers through your moss.
dark men who force you to kneel between umber legs
as they brush your hair and rub you dry with rough terry towels.
men who spread your legs in the light
pour plum wine into chalice and drink.
i love dark old men—tricks who tremble fingers like flame
worshiping what needs to be worshiped
taking care of more than business
filling their hands mouths eyes souls needs
finding the place rosepink liquid cleft to stroke past memory
dark old men who drip sweat and grind "talk to me"
drip sweat and grind "tell me about it"
grind "you're my whore. say it—say it."

WANDA COLEMAN ON PENNY GASAWAY'S Dark Old Men

Despite the best efforts of contemporary African American poets and writers, rarely have I seen a more authentic portrayal of a certain type of black man than in this remarkable poem by fifty-seven-year-old Penny Gasaway, who happens not to be black—her fraternal grandmother belongs to the Karok tribe.

I discovered this poem when we appeared in the same issue of *Pacific Review* in 1984. I found her images so wrenchingly true and crisp, I could smell the flesh rise from the page. I have known many such dark old men—play uncles, preachers, lovers, friends—as legends, and each time I read the poem, I am transported to those "attic rooms," although not all of the rooms are attics. Some are the back house, the shed, the room upstairs, the way-back-over-thattaway. I see them hunched over cards, playing Coon-Can, Bid Whist, or Tonk. I see the rise of chiseled, hairless chests, the roll of hooch-reddened eyes, sleek lanky arms with lengthy fingers arcing for a lock of hair or to lift a shade. I can smell night come to morning—the odors of sweat, cigarette smoke, and bleakness rising from an infinite variety of fabrics—all of them worn, having seen too many pressings, or wrinkled from being slept in. I squint through the dimness to find a decades-deep ulceration on the soul.

These men are old even when they're young.

Gasaway has captured the Black man-made-passive under an oppression (chronically high unemployment, high mortality rate, high health-related deaths, high imprisonment rate) that has robbed him of virtually all but his sexual prowess. His pain is as old as the maafa or Middle Passage. At some point in American history, between the breeding plantations and the lynchings, certain tribal customs dictated that women, aside from child-rearing and homemaking, conduct the business of the tribe, from raising crops to hunting to warfare, while the men talked philosophy and religion and made and enacted laws. It is my theory that this truncated tribal circumstance, once its practitioners were exported to American soil, coincided with the subculture of the sex trade in which the woman, by force or by circumstance, bore responsibility for supporting and/or protecting the man.

Having survived being torn from his origins, deprived of his tongue and his history, this new American Black man would soon learn to exploit his masculinity and his understanding of women. Not necessarily a flesh-peddler, he is stylistically the opposite "of," though kin to, what is infamous as the urban pimp, hustler, or misogynistic player known for the hard mack (come-on) and his ostentatiousness. Often "Dark Old Men" merely take many wives plus or minus ceremony. They are not necessarily malicious, but good and patient lovers with weighty walks, lopes, or gaits, their words spoken deep in the throat with a begging quality that leaves a woman feeling charmed, spellbound, or captured. Fulfillment is their crusade. Women may share them willingly. A seasoned older version of Jules (Samuel Jackson) from *Pulp Fiction* would be this type of man. Al Green's rhythm-and-roses stage persona is this type of man. Robert Johnson may have been this type of man. The history of the blues sings the lives of these men, who live outside the mainstream culture.

After meeting Penny Gasaway and getting her permission to read the poem whenever I chose, we lost touch in the mid-'90s. After a search, I recently found her still in pursuit of the muse. Raised in San Mateo and Belmont, California, she attended Los Angeles City College, received her B.A. from California State University San Bernardino, and her M.F.A. from U.C.–Irvine in 1988. A ten-year resident of South Central L.A.—my home turf—she has five children and one living husband. ("I've buried 2 in 15 years.")

One more thing about this poem, without stepping on Gasaway's powerful closing lines: the key word used, the noun, has to be heard beyond its mundane meaning. Because the manner in which this word is spoken is ritual-like, an evocation. The way *this kind* of man says *that kind* of word transforms it into something vital, beautiful, and sustaining—far above its otherwise mundane and denigrating connotation.

Adulterated

JACK GILBERT

Bella fica! (beautiful fig, fine sex) the whore said
in the back streets of Livorno, proudly slapping
her groin when the man tried to get the price down.
Braddock, the heavyweight champion of the world,
when Joe Louis was destroying him, blood spraying
and his manager between rounds wanting to stop
the fight, said, I won the title in the ring,
I'm going to lose it in the ring. And, after more
damage, did. Therefore does the wind keep blowing
that holds this great Earth in the air.
For this the birds sing sometimes without purpose.
We value the soiled old theaters because of what
sometimes happens there. Berlin in the Thirties.
There were flowers all around Jesus in his agony
at Gethsemane. The Lord sees everything, and sees
that it is good despite everything. The manger
was filthy. The women at Dachau knew they were about
to be gassed when they pushed back the Nazi guard
who wanted to die with them, saying he must live.
And sang for a little while after the doors closed.

Jack Gilbert, having won the Yale Series of Younger Poets competition in 1962 for *Views of Jeopardy,* has since published two volumes of poems, *Monolithos* (1982) and *The Great Fires* (1992). The mastery of an art form, Ezra Pound argued, is the work of a lifetime. Gilbert's small body of work is the work of a master and the work of a lifetime. Bearing a kinship to Pound and to the Greek poet Yannis Ritsos, Gilbert masters both the lyric and the epic modes, creating a new modality: the vision and voice of an epic radiant within the confines and subtractions of a lyric utterance. We have not attended to his poems with the same intensity he brings to them.

I would usually use such words as austere, minimal, and ascetic to describe Gilbert's poems, stripped as they are of any flourishes and worn down to their stark elements, it seems, by the erosion of time: geologic, mythic, historic, as well as by the time and labor of an individual life. The locus of many of Gilbert's poems is a solitary place, a hillside in Greece, for instance, a landscape composed of dust, moonlight, the distant sound of goat bells, and the self that speaks the poems speaks out of isolation, out of exile, stranded, islanded—a Prospero without his magic. In "Threshing the Fire," he writes: "I would burrow into stone, into iron," as he hears "cicadas on the olive trees rage in brevity." Between brevity and a thousand years is the human life: marooned in time, lived second by second, joy by joy, grief by grief, loss by loss, as a moment forgotten, a moment remembered.

In "Adulterated," as in several poems in *The Great Fires,* more and more is added to the poem rather than erased, more and more is pulled into its gravity: the sacred and profane, tenderness and cruelty, song and silence, dignity and degradation, distances and intimacies. Which of these adulterate, we might ask ourselves? Which of these offers a falsified vision or a true vision of human baseness and human compassion?

Poems are not usually in the business of providing answers. If this poem offers an answer, it balances precariously on the fulcrum of a "therefore." If this poem offers an answer, it might be glimpsed through the ragged chinks between defeat and glory, nostalgia and bitterness, Gethsemene and Dachau, the sacrifice and the slaughter.

Birthday Cake

PAUL GOODMAN

Now isn't it time
when the candles on the icing
are one two too many
too many to blow out
too many to count too many
isn't it time to give up this ritual?

although the fiery crown
fluttering on the chocolate
and through the darkened room advancing
is still the most loveliest sight
among our savage folk
that have few festivals.

But the thicket is too hot and thick
and isn't it time, isn't it time
when the fires are too many
to eat the fire and not the cake
and drip the fires from my teeth
as once I had my hot hot youth.

TONY HOAGLAND ON PAUL GOODMAN'S Birthday Cake

Paul Goodman's "Birthday Cake" does almost everything I would ask a wonderful poem to do: it couples raw emotional force with the sophistication of a cultivated, penetrating intellect. What's more, these complex, distinct powers of the self—Id and Superego—are given voice alternately—left hand, right hand—in the course of the poem. As a result, the portrayal of human nature is rich, complex, tiered; we see the intelligence of passion and the compassion of intellect. Bursting through at the end is a climactic, satisfying integration of rage and sanity, responsibility and spontaneity, self-serving impulses and culture-consciousness. "Birthday Cake" plays the whole chord.

Paul Goodman, now a rather forgotten figure, was one of the amazing, charismatic men-of-letters—it seems there were many of them then—of the 1950s and '60s. He wrote books on city planning, psychology, radical educational philosophy, and everything else, and he did it all well. He moved smoothly between bohemian and academic realms, raised a family and had a simultaneous homosexual life, preached anarchist politics and wrote literary criticism. I think poetry was a sideline for Goodman, the private practice of a passionate, cultivated person—but he was prolific, talented, natural, and occasionally he would write the perfect poem. He published a lot in his time, but it was not the center of his reputation. He himself said that he did not try for individual poems, but for an attitude about living. I learned of Goodman's poems from Hayden Carruth's great anthology *The Spirit Which Moves Within Us,* and from an essay by Carruth which appeared many years ago in *American Poetry Review.* Goodman has a half-dozen poems worth memorizing for their vitality, skill, and truth.

"Birthday Cake" demonstrates how relaxed, improvisational, and expressive a strong poem can be. Not in the least cerebral but hugely smart, it fully inhabits feeling but has a shifting perspective on that feeling. Of course, the speaker of the poem is an aging man, confronting the daunting ceremony of the birthday cake. The sweetness is no longer sweet because it heralds the approach of death.

The first stanza opens with the authoritative, rhetorical question, a speech-gesture which willfully implies its own answer: Yes, it is time to give up this ritual. Rhetorical openings sometimes seem overcontrolled. Yet the plaintive, repetitive simplicity of Goodman's vocabulary here, and the broken-down, run-on syntax illustrate that the speaker is also out of control, driven by feverish feeling. The rushing, plaintive phrases are the unpunctuated outcry of the child-self: *I-don't-wanna-I-don't-wanna,* unconcerned with grammatical correctness. The grammar of the Id is always simple: subject-verb, and the dominant energy of stanza one is Id-ish.

The second stanza of Goodman's poem is one big qualifying clause, beginning with the conjunction "although." It is counter-thought, a distinctly different altitude from stanza one. If the first stanza is urgent with feeling and minimal in information, the second stanza is packed with information and formal in tone. Grammatically elaborate, sophisticated in temper and technique, it is a lyrical essay in six lines.

What is the substance of that essay? That the rituals of culture are ancient and indispensable. In part, this message is borne by imagery. The "fiery crown fluttering" carries not just a perceptual richness but a rich evocation of cultural history: the feudal resonances of crowns and festivals, not to mention fire, are communal and sacred. And the dark room itself suggests a cavernous, pre-electric setting, where savage folk (and children) gather for collective warmth and ceremony.

Diction shifts upward in stanza two, as does syntax. The syntax of stanza two is processional and elaborate, as it needs to be to carry so much information; most wonderful is the iambic, formal inversion of line nine: not "moving through the dark room," but "and through the darkened room advancing." This formalizing of language signifies a psychic transformation, too. In this stanza, the aging speaker psychologically rises above his petty self-concern and considers the welfare of the culture as a whole, which he sympathetically recognizes is "savage" and therefore in need of preservation and sponsorship. Is it coincidence that the "small" self is transcended in the most formalized speech of the poem? No.

Just a vestige of the child-self remains visible in stanza two, in that double-superlative adjective, "most loveliest sight"—a moment of affectionate gush which communicates the simple appeal of fire and chocolate and a dark room.

The final stanza of "Birthday Cake" descends again to the level of the plaintive, imperative Id, into the "thicket" of intense emotion, back to the repetitious, pell-mell anxious child-voice. Again, as in stanza one, the speech becomes largely monosyllabic. But in stanza three, the anxiety slowly, painfully transforms from self-pity to anger, and the psychic helplessness is brilliantly transmuted into a formulation of action—to eat the fire and not the cake.

In this imaginative act, this bursting-through, the poem resoundingly answers the question it began with: Is it time to give up this ritual? No—rather, it is time to *revise* the ritual in a glorious, self-destructive and vitality-affirming spectacle.

This promised act is at once comic, exhibitionistic, and triumphant. The aging king of the ego eats his crown, affirms his virility, and concedes his absurdity all at once. This too is a ceremony. It is a triumph of Id and Superego at once, a home run for self and culture.

Guide to Marine Mammals and Sentence Structure

ADAM HAMMER

1. Beginning With An Exclamation
Panico! I badly need an oat, or something! said the
bewildered marine mammal.

2. Subject-Predicate-Preposition Phrase
A thousand thousand marine mammal helicopters
screeched into the night.

3. Compound Sentence
The Marine halted, then wrote _____ in the fetus's
left-hand margin.

4. Compound Direct Object
The Marine ate a mammal, and a Mallomar, and an axe.

5. Complicated Sentence
The mammals gathered on the stinking steamship and
discussed the Ancient Mariner, then leaped into the life-
rickshaw to search the marine-stained toast for mamma-
lade, all the while realizing that the new-neo captain had
drained all the pseudo-animals, of which many of them
had heard, and / or carefully elongating the fez.

6. Parallel Construction
The Teeth-Mammal was sad, and cried real teargas, and
was naked at last.

7. Dietetic Sentence
The mammal was over-marinated; we ate up the bark;
the bison and buffalo squared off in the glen.

8. Perverted Sentence
The filthy Marine went AWOL to see Melba of the
Mammals bend over backwards, a strange sight.

9. Sentence With 'Velcro' In It
Old, poisonous Juan had a fondness for Velcro.

10. Sad Sentence
In the Chinese prison, old mammals crept, their arms full
of gills.

JIM DANIELS ON ADAM HAMMER'S Guide to Marine Mammals and
    Sentence Structure

Adam Hammer died in a car wreck in the early '80s. Since his death,
I have seen none of his poems in print, though he was writing poems
back in the late '70s that in many ways were ahead of the poetry curve.
It would be too simple to label Hammer a surrealist poet. When I pick
up the various anthologies of contemporary poetry and see the various
styles and "schools," the only one Hammer doesn't seem to fit into is
"New Formalism." And when I look back to Hammer's work, I find his
poems are better and more original than much of what I find in those
collections.

In addition to being funny and outrageously surreal, Hammer often
plays with words the way some of the language poets do. This particu-
lar poem shows Hammer's love of words as objects. He revels in their
sounds and shapes—"Juan," "Mallomar," "fez," "Velcro," "fetus"—and
places them in odd, ridiculous combinations—"new-neo, pseudo-
mammals, marine-stained toast," etc. Hammer riffs on both the idea of
"marine" and the idea of "mammal": "mammalade," "Ancient Mariner,"
"Marine," "marinated," free-associating madly within the logic-grid of
the instructions of the poem.

Like Walt Whitman on acid, Hammer's poems are wildly inclu-
sive, embracing America in all its weirdness and perversity. He relied
more heavily on pop culture references and proper names than most

poets writing in the late '70s, although those references are now matter-of-factly sprinkled through a great deal of contemporary poetry. *Déjà Everything,* the book from which this poem comes, is dedicated not to lover or family, but to Willie Mays. In it, Hammer references Mallomars, Velcro, the Vancouver Canucks, Dots, Volkswagens, Vicks Cough Silencers, etc.

Everything was a target for Hammer's sharp wit. In this poem, he slips in a little dig at Robert Bly's *The Teeth-Mother Naked at Last* in section six, and the whole poem is in part a send-up of the grammar-obsessed composition classes many writers have taught and continue to teach.

The joy of reading Hammer's poems comes from strapping yourself in and going along for the ride. Hammer's sitting next to you, his seatbelt unbuckled, laughing. The remarkable thing about this poem is that the reader does arrive somewhere; the "sad sentence" *is* clearly sad, and resonates off the poem's title. For all his indirectness and strangeness, he can pull the elephant out of the hat at the end.

I knew Adam Hammer when we were both in graduate school in Bowling Green, Ohio. When Skylab was going to fall to earth, we decided to have a Skylab party, so we drove up to Detroit with the idea of picking up a World War I helmet I knew was in my parents' basement. We ended up going to a Detroit Tigers baseball game and then to a bar called The Zoo. Only Adam Hammer could get kicked out of a bar called The Zoo. Afterward, we stopped by my parents' house at some ungodly hour to get the helmet. My mother got up and made us grilled cheese sandwiches to sober us up while Hammer explained to her why he thought newspapers should be printed on meat. The spontaneous free-association of that night, and of his remark to my mother, evokes the same energy that I find in Hammer's poems. They have a "stand-up" quality to them, an implied performance aspect, as if they were written to be read aloud. Unfortunately, he's not around to read them to us.

Perhaps Hammer's poetry has been ignored because of his early, untimely death, or because the book was published by a small press. Or maybe it seemed not to take itself seriously enough in the post-Vietnam era.

I own a handful of books that cause me to panic if I misplace them—*Déjà Everything* is one of them. James Tate, in his blurb for *Déjà Everything,* wrote: "Adam Hammer doesn't sound like anyone else." Twenty-five years later this is still true, and reason enough for us to take another look at his poems. He was funny when most American poetry wasn't. He continues to be funny. James Wright once said that the problem with American surrealist poets is that they don't get the joke. Adam Hammer always got the joke.

[On your midnight pallet lying]

A. E. HOUSMAN

On your midnight pallet lying,
    Listen, and undo the door:
Lads that waste the light in sighing
    In the dark should sigh no more;
Night should ease a lover's sorrow;
Therefore, since I go to-morrow,
    Pity me before.

In the land to which I travel,
    The far dwelling, let me say—
Once, if here the couch is gravel,
    In a kinder bed I lay,
And the breast the darnel smothers
Rested once upon another's
    When it was not clay.

Even in his lifetime, A. E. Housman was the subject of mystified and sometimes malicious speculation. How could a man so famously repressed and reticent, a renowned teacher who never deigned to look at his students, a solitary man who loathed the company of strangers and even in a room with his few friends was often uncomfortable, an arrogant, austere, aloof and caustic man given to forbidding silences—how could this man have written *A Shropshire Lad,* a book beloved by generations of readers, a book of passionate tenderness, of extraordinary pathos and daring, of longings and sighs and memories that echo and ache in a reader's heart even today? It was easy to poke fun at him. Frank Harris said he looked like "an undertaker's mute." Max Beerbohm said he resembled "an absconding cashier." Even Housman's sister Clemence, when she'd first read *A Shropshire Lad,* mocked him: "Alfred has a heart!"

Indeed he did, and one of the strangest in literary history. He was twelve when his beloved mother died, and from that moment on he hid his feelings, abjured any belief in God, and was haunted by an unappeasable yearning not unlike that cloudy, Romantic feeling that suffuses Leopardi's "L'infinito." At Oxford, he met the man he would love for the rest of his life, Moses Jackson. There was never any sex, but Housman may once have bared his heart, at which declaration Jackson fled the rooms they shared . . . to marriage, to India, to remotest Canada. They kept in cordial but infrequent touch as old mates, and saw one another only a couple of times later, but the flame in Housman's soul burned undiminished down the decades. Housman could later write wistfully about the situation. Here is one such poem, published posthumously:

> Shake hands, we never shall be friends, all's over;
> > I only vex you the more I try.
> All's wrong that ever I've done or said,
> And nought to help it in this dull head:
> > Shake hands, here's luck, goodbye.
>
> But if you come to a road where danger
> > Or guilt or anguish or shame's to share,

Be good to the lad that loves you true
And the soul that was born to die for you,
   And whistle and I'll be there.

That is a characteristic Housman poem: plain-spoken but measured and elegant, melancholy but stoic, a message posted from what he once called "the land of lost content." To pluck out the heart of its mystery, however, one would have to focus closely on the shared threats listed in the second stanza: *danger, guilt, anguish, shame.* They are the lot of the closeted homosexual.

A Shropshire Lad is a sequence of sixty-three numbered poems, most of them simply identified by their Roman numeral. ("On your midnight pallet lying" is number XI.) The two books of poems Housman published during his life were each written in sudden spurts of creative energy. During the first three months of 1895, he wrote almost all of the poems in *A Shropshire Lad.* (The book appeared the next year; Housman had to offer a subvention to the publisher and never received a royalty.) It might be added that 1895 was also the year of the Oscar Wilde trials, and that same year—in an incident widely reported—a naval cadet at Woolwich, realizing he was homosexual, shot himself. Housman wrote about it with a bitter irony:

   Shot? so quick, so clean an ending?
      Oh that was right, lad, that was brave:
   Yours was not an ill for mending,
      'Twas best to take it to the grave.

Wilde himself, after his release from prison, was sent a copy of Housman's book, and he praised it as "terribly realistic." In a way, Housman's poems are Wilde's glittery paradoxes turned darkly inside out. Though rarely direct or literal, Housman struck his own *De Profundis* note, and savagely attacked the hypocrisies of the age. One satirical poem has a man taken to prison "for the nameless and abominable colour of his hair." Another ends more ruefully:

   I, a stranger and afraid
   In a world I never made.
   They will be master, right or wrong;
   Though both are foolish, both are strong.

And since, my soul, we cannot fly
To Saturn nor to Mercury,
Keep we must, if keep we can,
These foreign laws of God and man.

But the terrible realism Wilde noted is finally an emotional realism: no poet before Housman or since has written so exquisitely of the pain of separation. I say *exquisitely* because he cultivates and cherishes the very anguish he dramatizes. Near the end of Moses Jackson's life, Housman wrote to remind him that "you are largely responsible for my writing poetry." Thirty-five years he had loved this man: his torment, his only hope, his muse.

"On your midnight pallet lying" is a strong example of the eerie romance Housman enacted in his work. It is about two dead men, though you would not guess that at first. The opening stanza, with its admonitory *shoulds,* seems a traditional complaint: the lover, albeit this time another man, excluded from the beloved's bed and begging entry. It is a poem that might as well begin: Had I but world enough and time. But the second stanza startles the reader into a new awareness. As soon as we stumble on "the far dwelling," and realize the speaker is about to die, or has just died, the poem's tone changes. Are we meant to take this literally, or as an extreme conceit? Are the gravel and grass (in earlier versions, Housman has written first "cere-cloth," then "tombstone," then "knot-grass," before settling on "darnel," itself a species of rye grass) now the ghost's bed and blanket, or morbidly pastoral images of an emotional life-in-death? Only Hardy before him wrote in the language of ghosts so powerfully. (It might be noted that Housman was a pallbearer at Hardy's funeral.) The next-to-last line of the poem is the one Housman changed the most. It initially read "Breathed against a happy lover's," making explicit the relationship between the two men. Then, shifting the imagined intimacy from mouth to heart, he wrote: "Beat one night upon a lover's." Then the calmer "Rested once upon a lover's." Does the final change—to "another's"—back away from a more compelling explicitness? Perhaps. Yet the delicacy and desperation of the less specific "another's" has, to my ear, a peculiar melancholy. The other's breast was once alive, but now is clay—a trope, I suppose, on the heart of stone.

I return to this poem over and over again because it yields so many readings, so many pangs and possibilities. The "far dwelling" is, I take it at times, Housman's desk, his single bed, his imagination, his loneliness. Henry James, in a letter, once declared that "the essential loneliness of my life" was its core, and plumbed deeper than any other fact or sensation: "Deeper about me, at any rate, than anything else: deeper than my 'genius,' deeper than my 'discipline,' deeper than my pride, deeper, above all, than the deep countermining of art." Housman is the great poet of loneliness. Not of solitude, when one withdraws from life. But loneliness, when life withdraws from one. The Might-have-been and Never-can-be are Housman's pen and ink. His nostalgia is sorrowing, his endurance harrowing. His poems, apparently so easy to read, their rhythms and rhymes glacially ordered, still slide effortlessly between layers of meaning and implication. Their chiseled bleakness stands as a monument to the unlived life, the emptiness that fills the heart's chambers, where anyone's midnight pallet is set.

White Poems

LANGSTON HUGHES

Island

Wave of sorrow,
Do not drown me now:

I see the island
Still ahead somehow.

I see the island
And its sands are fair:

Wave of sorrow
Take me there.

Moonlight Night: Carmel

Tonight the waves march
In long ranks
Cutting the darkness
With their silver shanks
Cutting the darkness
And kissing the moon
And beating the land's
Edge into a swoon.

Winter Moon

How thin and sharp is the moon tonight!
How thin and sharp and ghostly white
Is the slim curved crook of the moon tonight

LYNN EMANUEL ON LANGSTON HUGHES'S White Poems

In 1997, the year my father was dying, I discovered the *Selected Poems of Langston Hughes* in a newsstand in the Newark airport. Later, in an article for the *Boston Globe,* I described my surprise at reading the sweep of those small lyrics, which I had been used to seeing scattered in anthologies, and this, I discovered, meant that I had not been reading Hughes at all. "Island," plucked from its context, represents Hughes's work about as well as "I'm Nobody! Who Are You?" does Dickinson's. Hughes's cosmology unfolds in the unorthodox form of small lyric poems strung one upon another with seeming casualness. "Island" functions as a poignant lyric about sorrow and hope whose general pronouncements could pertain to my feelings about the death of my father. While this reading is acceptable, it does not account for the galvanizing effect Hughes's short poems now have on me. It does not allow for Hughes's despondent genius.

Anthologized, Hughes's small poems are reduced to the lower case of conventional wisdom. The anthology (or textbook) often neutralizes Hughes by allowing his lyric poems to be read as "universal" (i.e., of a certain comforting significance even to the white reader); and/or as a collection of artifacts of historical interest because of the way they incorporated the blues; and/or for their celebration of Negritude. For instance, in the most recent edition of *An Introduction to Poetry* (Longman; ed. X. J. Kennedy and Dana Gioia), a reader comes to "Island" after this introduction to Hughes: "A strikingly versatile writer . . . Hughes also became a tireless promoter of African American culture, crisscrossing the United States on speaking tours."

Selected Poems, which Hughes himself collected and assembled shortly before his death, is a bracing correction to these conventions of reading. *Selected* reveals that each poem, like a cell, carries within it the structure of the larger organism. Thus, a reader cannot access even a seemingly straightforward poem, such as "Island," without understanding it in the context of Hughes's symbology rather than merely in the context of history. What has largely been unacknowledged in Hughes is his essentially tragic and Manichean view of race. In *Selected Poems,* one finds Hughes's assertion of the murderous and co-equal power of the white. For Hughes, white is as "natural" as black, evil as "natural" as good. The brevity of his lyrics foreclose on the possibilities of explanation or mitigation of this "fact."

"Moonlight Night: Carmel" is typical of Hughes's tragic world, in which the seemingly dispassionate narrator observes the "natural" horror of the racial universe. The tragedy in Hughes's position manifests in his near appreciation of, or captivation by, that which undermines him. The final discomforting verb, "swoon," suggests that his experience of the annihilating "cutting," and "kissing" and "beating" white borders on daze, or rapture. The near loss of consciousness at whiteness in the world—atavistic, brutal, inhuman, murderous—shares an affinity with the experience of the erotic.

To return to "Island" and its fair, oneiric sands: no island in Hughes is "fair." In the context of *Selected Poems,* "Island" touches the white sands, white waves, and margins of all Hughes's other islands and coasts and is unmistakably "tainted" by its context; the "silver shanks," scythe of the moon, and other manifestations and paraphernalia of evil share the sinister paleness of Hughes's cosmology. "Island" in an anthology is "about hope." In the context of *Selected Poems,* "Island" is a poem suicidal with despair. Faced with possible present extermination by woe ("Do not drown me now"), the narrator imagines the possibility of a future: "I see the island . . . Take me there." But the possible future is implicated in, not separated from, the racial universe embodied in "fair sands." The narrator, poised between "Do not drown me now" and "I see the island . . . Take me there," must make a tragic choice between a present or future extermination: drown now or later.

It is not only the deliberate understatement of Hughes's small poems that—oddly—makes them inaccessible by making them appear transparent, it is their tragic stance towards race. Hughes's poems subvert and question the hegemony of American pragmatism. They do not fit within the current ethos of activism. His poems present no "cure" for racism.

This work needs to be rescued from the generally complacent readings it is given. These exceptional small poems are still missing in the larger appreciation of Hughes's poetry and absent from contemporary American poetry's conversations about race. What is required are readers who are willing to "miss" the obvious point and to read these poems in the tragic and fatalistic context Hughes himself imagined for them when he compiled his *Selected Poems*.

The Fish, the Man, and the Spirit

LEIGH HUNT

TO A FISH

You strange, astonished-looking, angle-faced,
    Dreary-mouthed, gaping wretches of the sea,
    Gulping salt-water everlastingly,
Cold-blooded, though with red your blood be graced,
And mute, though dwellers in the roaring waste;
    And you, all shapes beside, that fishy be,—
    Some round, some flat, some long, all devilry,
Legless, unloving, infamously chaste:—

O scaly, slippery, wet, swift, staring wights,
　　What is't ye do? What life lead? eh, dull goggles?
How do ye vary your vile days and nights?
　　How pass your Sundays? Are ye still but joggles
In ceaseless wash? Still nought but gapes, and bites,
　　And drinks, and stares, diversified with boggles?

A FISH ANSWERS

Amazing monster! that, for aught I know,
　　With the first sight of thee didst make our race
　　For ever stare! O flat and shocking face,
Grimly divided from the breast below!
Thou that on dry land horribly dost go
　　With a split body and most ridiculous pace,
　　Prong after prong, disgracer of all grace,
Long-useless-finned, haired, upright, unwet, slow!

O breather of unbreathable, sword-sharp air,
　　How canst exist? How bear thyself, thou dry
And dreary sloth? What particle canst share
　　Of the only blessed life, the watery?
I sometimes see of ye an actual *pair*
　　Go by! linked fin by fin! most odiously.

THE FISH TURNS INTO A MAN, AND THEN
INTO A SPIRIT, AND AGAIN SPEAKS

Indulge thy smiling scorn, if smiling still,
　　O man! And loathe, but with a sort of love;
　　For difference must its use by difference prove,
And, in sweet clang, the sphere with music fill.
One of the spirits am I, that at his will
　　Live in whate'er has life—fish, eagle, dove—
　　No hate, no pride, beneath nought, nor above,
A visitor of the rounds of God's sweet skill.

Man's life is warm, glad, sad, 'twixt loves and graves,
  Boundless in hope, honoured with pangs austere,
Heaven-gazing; and his angel-wings he craves:—
  The fish is swift, small-needing, vague yet clear,
A cold, sweet, silver life, wrapped in round waves,
  Quickened with touches of transporting fear.

The Fish, the Man, and the Spirit

Leigh Hunt was a busy man-of-letters, well known in his time (1784–1859) as a poet, critic, editor, general shaker-upper and seeder of the arts, and an acquaintance of many, if not most, of London's important writers and thinkers. His various literary projects, both successful and failed; his gently shabby-bohemian lifestyle and difficult marriage; his years of hobnobbing with a community of seminal artists and philosophers; and his almost naively unworldly ways (and financial distresses) . . . these are all the grist of literary legend (he appears tellingly in *Neighboring Lives,* the historical novel by Disch and Naylor that enters the social circle of Thomas and Jane Carlyle). But the poem of his under consideration here stands—as I believe most fine writing does—independent of the need for any biographical support.

Occasionally some piece of writing seems to embody a future sensibility, as if a time traveler had journeyed into history and inadvertently left a poem or a novel on those wayback shores. That would be technologically marvelous—the traveler, I mean, and his centuries-eating machine. But I think the other possibility, the psychological one, is even more marvelous: that someone's mind in past-time A, against all odds and anomalously, can resonate in empathy with our current-moment Zeitgeist.

One example—minor, but endearingly charming—is Leigh Hunt's poem "The Fish, the Man, and the Spirit," an inspired piece of intelligent whimsy that blends a serious "nature poem" from the guidebook of the Romantics with a few jiggy Edward Lear molecules; provides that mix with a weird, presiding "spirit" out of William Blake (by way of Walt

Disney); and charges the whole concoction with a jolt of dream logic straight out of Borges or Isabel Allende or Gabriel García Márquez.

Where *did* this triplet of sonnets come from? Its sense of ecological codependence—its implicit holistic vision of an Earth where the life-force flows with equal worth through every partum of life—is less that of the anthropocentric Great-Chain-of-Being mentality that would still have been thundered from pulpits in Hunt's own day, and more of the mindset driving Greenpeace. "Equal rights for Fishes!"—long before even the women's suffrage movement had started to profitably coalesce. Fishes. It's a big big deal when Wordsworth's manifesto asks for using the language of lower-class men and women in our literature . . . and here's Hunt asking—before the Starship Enterprise was the scantest of dreams—to mind-meld with the fishes.

And he does great, detailed, empathetic justice to that finny tribe— those last three lines are a wonder. Keats's nightingale (of his famous Ode) is only the idea of a bird: we never hear it make the slightest real-world rustles in its bough; we never stop to think that it mates and preens and craps in fear of predators. But Hunt's fish is (just as D. H. Lawrence's fish will be, a bit later on in the poetry timeline) a credible creature, with dreams and stinks of its own. And Keats doesn't linger all that leisurely in the head of his twittering bird: he's in, he ponders Grand Stuff, and he's out again. But Hunt, although his poem is more brief, is clearly in for the long haul: he's interested in the actual nitty-gritty, silt-and-milt, *fishness* of things.

Keats's is surely the greater poem, for a host of reasons. But I wouldn't want to do without Hunt's mini-tour of the levels of Creation, his tri-fold letter of love to existence, that carries such interesting intellectual baggage and yet has the eldritch sparkle of something discovered under a leaf in the deeps of a fairy forest. It's like . . . what *is* it like? Like sitting around with Thoreau in his cabin, discussing the glories of Nature in a slow and steady way, while through the window one sees a parade of drunken Monty-Python vicars reciting favorite sonnets into the air.

I admire the wide embrace of its cuckoo cast of characters, and (for this is a small trilogy, with a plan—a shape, a direction) the way that, after the bickering gets finished, they contribute toward one final, abiding tenderness. I admire the democracy of voices—let's say: evolution's version of an Ellis Island of voices, as lyrically scripted by Gilbert and Sullivan. I admire the way those voices, high and low, predate the brilliant twentieth century crazy-quilt chorus of John Berryman's *Dream Songs*. I admire Hunt's ability to wed so smoothly the skin of formal constraint with its unlikely partner, the zany personality of a 1940s Hollywood screwball comedy. And I particularly admire the aerial currents of "magic realism" on which the "spirit" is borne, as it clears its ethereal throat and brushes the particolor dusts from its garments—dusts that it picked up, I swear, a day earlier in the future as it flew through a *shtetl* painted by Chagall in his signature rose and sea-blue.

As Many Questions as Answers

LAURA (RIDING) JACKSON

What is to start?
It is to have feet to start with.
What is to end?
It is to have nothing to start again with,
And not to wish.

What is to see?
It is to know in part.
What is to speak?
It is to add part to part
And make a whole
Of much or little.
What is to whisper?
It is to make soft
The greed of speaking faster
Than is substance for.
What is to cry out?
It is to make gigantic
Where speaking cannot last long.

What is to be?
It is to bear a name.
What is to die?
It is to be name only.
And what is to be born?
It is to choose the enemy self
To learn impossibility from.
And what is to have hope?
Is it to choose a god weaker than self,
And pray for compliments?

What is to ask?
It is to find an answer.
What is to answer?
Is it to find a question?

BIN RAMKE ON LAURA (RIDING) JACKSON'S
As Many Questions as Answers

I know of only one poet who took poetry so seriously that she finally repudiated it. Sometime around 1940, Laura (Riding) Jackson stopped writing poetry, much as Marcel Duchamp chose to stop making art objects and instead turned to chess playing as a kind of performance art (and was not particularly good at it). Jackson chose to write only a kind of philosophy and occasional polemical pieces explaining her rejection of poetry, even at times as prefaces to anthologized reprinting of her poems, the choice *not* to create as itself the act of the artist. Why? The short answer is that she found poetry failed as a medium for universal truth.

Having been famously (passionately and nearly fatally) allied with Robert Graves, having known and been known and praised by the major figures of early twentieth-century literature, Laura (Riding) Jackson's very name is a kind of history, an enactment and display of issues and betrayals, if read imaginatively. There are now biographies and critical texts that work wonders for our appreciation of her nuanced life and language, and I recommend them all. But I also recommend at least one poem that can be approached respectfully and read with a kind of naïveté, and which rewards all who enter it patiently. The title is itself a poem, "As Many Questions as Answers," especially after we have counted the questions and answers in the poem and discover that, after several exchanges, more or less direct, in which questions are answered declaratively, "What is to hope?" is answered with a question, and the twelfth question, the question of questions, is answered: "Is it to find a question?" Perhaps all questions are also answers, in which case the equation (as many questions as answers) holds.

And yet the poem is full of the physical, of the body, of pathos and passionate fears. "What is to start?/ It is to have feet to start with." Of course these "feet" may well be read as metrical feet, which might send us to counting syllables and marking stresses in this very poem. But the word might be read as those very human extremities with which we dance and walk, and which famously mark the bad off (no shoes) from the terribly bad off (no feet), and which are necessary for beginning even a journey of a thousand miles. And later, the achingly personal answer to the biggest, most abstract question imaginable: What is to be? It is to bear a name (consider the history of a Laura herself whose several successive last names she kept nearby, like pets or ex-lovers she couldn't quite bear to part with). Even the question following—"What is to die?"—doesn't contain the poignancy of this answer.

Laura (Riding) Jackson's work has, after her fairly recent death, enjoyed a revival among poets. Still, her name is hardly a household word, and this is in part her own choosing. What is the point of renouncing an art if you're going to become famous anyway? In some sense, it is right that all the elements of her life and art do not add up, that the accounting of her accomplishment and her proper place, canonically speaking, is doomed to perpetual provisional status. There will always be, in any good poetry, as many questions as answers, but rarely will their mere enumeration be as graceful, powerful, and suggestive as in this little poem.

Mummy of a Lady Named Jemutesonekh
XXI Dynasty

THOMAS JAMES

My body holds its shape. The genius is intact.
Will I return to Thebes? In that lost country
The eucalyptus trees have turned to stone.
Once, branches nudged me, dropping swollen blossoms,
And passionflowers lit my father's garden.
Is it still there, that place of mottled shadow,
The scarlet flowers breathing in the darkness?

I remember how I died. It was so simple!
One morning the garden faded. My face blacked out.
On my left side they made the first incision.
They washed my heart and liver in palm wine—
My lungs were two dark fruit they stuffed with spices.
They smeared my innards with a sticky unguent
And sealed them in a crock of alabaster.

My brain was next. A pointed instrument
Hooked it through my nostrils, strand by strand.
A voice swayed over me. I paid no notice.
For weeks my body swam in sweet perfume.
I came out scoured. I was skin and bone.
They lifted me into the sun again
And packed my empty skull with cinnamon.

They slit my toes; a razor gashed my fingertips.
Stitched shut at last, my limbs were chaste and valuable,
Stuffed with a paste of cloves and wild honey.
My eyes were empty, so they filled them up,
Inserting little nuggets of obsidian.
A basalt scarab wedged between my breasts
Replaced the tinny music of my heart.

Hands touched my sutures. I was so important!
They oiled my pores, rubbing a fragrance in.
An amber gum oozed down to soothe my temples.
I wanted to sit up. My skin was luminous,
Frail as the shadow of an emerald.
Before I learned to love myself too much,
My body wound itself in spools of linen.

Shut in my painted box, I am a precious object.
I wear a wooden mask. These are my eyelids,
Two flakes of bronze, and here is my new mouth,
Chiseled with care, guarding its ruby facets.
I will last forever. I am not impatient—
My skin will wait to greet its old complexions.
I'll lie here till the world swims back again.

When I come home the garden will be budding,
White petals breaking open, clusters of night flowers,
The far-off music of a tambourine.
A boy will pace among the passionflowers,
His eyes no longer two bruised surfaces.
I'll know the mouth of my young groom, I'll touch
His hands. Why do people lie to one another?

CAROL MUSKE-DUKES ON THOMAS JAMES' Mummy of a Lady
    Named Jemutesonekh XXI Dynasty

I first read this poem in *The American Poetry Anthology* (ed. Daniel
Halpern, 1975). I was taken with the work in this provocative collec-
tion, but this particular poem leaped out and startled me in that sud-
den, fearful, "zero at the bone" way, as if I'd heard a voice from beyond
death.

In a sense, I had. James was a suicide. After his first book of po-
ems, *Letters to a Stranger,* was published by Houghton-Mifflin in 1973, he
took his own life. James's biographical notes are brief: he graduated from
Northern Illinois University in 1968 and worked for a while in Chicago

as an employment counselor. He wrote a novel, *Picture Me Asleep,* that was dramatized as a play; he won the Theodore Roethke Prize for *Poetry Northwest* in 1969. He wrote a collection of poems in an unearthly voice and then he killed himself. He was twenty-seven.

The voice in "Mummy of a Lady" is utterly weightless, without the "gravity" of familiar context. Yet it is grounded in the still-humming, shifting-aura way that objects just hit by lightning are: it has been visited by the far border of existence. It appears to have accepted death. The voice is speaking as a spirit, yet it is a voice in love with the body, with the flesh. Just as the Egyptian priests who embalmed the bodies to be preserved as mummies were obsessed with anatomy and the rituals of anatomy—as well as with the idea of life after death—so too this voice respectfully intones: "They slit my toes; a razor gashed my fingertips." The tone echoes slightly the New Testament statements of the murdered, crucified Christ—"And they cast lots for my clothes."

The voice in the poem seems expectant. It appears to believe in eternal life, in life's renewal. One day the body will live again, thanks to the power of ritual. But the horror resident in this expectancy surfaces not long after we take in the last astonishing line, just after the description of the return of the Lady to her lover, her "young groom:" "Why do people lie to one another?" The question appears a little innocuous at first, but then we understand the mummy has succumbed to a familiar lie of hope, that its description of the body's return is a kind of send-up of the Christian resurrection myth. It is a refusal of death after all, not an acceptance. The dead body is beautified the way the living beautify their bodies. In this case, "My skin will wait to greet its old complexion."

The lie of hope, of life going on, is the real subject here. And I don't think the author believes that life will go on. All the precious jewels, all the attentions of prayer and process, will not bring back what is lost. A beautiful young woman has died, she has lost her life, her lover. All the elaborate cosmeticizing, the fetishizing of the mortuary, cannot return her breath. This terrible longing, caught between dimensions, out of time, breaks the reader's heart. This is a spirit haunting the body, not continuing to live within it. The poet has articulated, it seems to me, a horror: the possibility of consciousness beyond death with no further prospect of embodiment of that consciousness. Or the lie of the projection of this voice—beamed from the dead to the living.

On the other hand, the statement at the poem's end could simply be one of quiet despair. After creating the elaborate "brocade" (as Philip Larkin called religious belief), the poem suddenly slashes through the fiction that tempts us all with its "dressing up" of death. We ask ourselves, as he does: "Why *do* people lie to one another?"

Yet in another sense, James has resurrected his subject. Neglected though he has been, his arresting poem lives on in consciousness each time it is rediscovered and read. What might be mistaken for "ghoulish" details of embalming reverberate with power and beauty in the astonishing particulars. The poem itself is the "body" of the mummy—re-endowed with life. That's the comforting view, at any rate.

Radi os

RONALD JOHNSON

RADI   OS
  O I
O

           tree
         into the World,

                 Man

              the chosen

Rose out of Chaos:

            song,

*The first lines of Milton's poem with words canceled
(in effect) by Ronald Johnson.*

~~PARADISE LOST~~
~~BOOK~~ I
~~Of Man's first disobedience, and the fruit~~
~~Of that forbidden~~ tree ~~whose mortal taste~~
~~Brought death~~ into the World, ~~and all our woe,~~
~~With loss of Eden, till one greater~~ Man
~~Restore us, and regain the blissful seat,~~
~~Sing, Heavenly Muse, that, on the secret top~~
~~Of Oreb, or of Sinai, didst inspire~~
~~That shepherd who first taught~~ the chosen ~~seed~~
~~In the beginning how the heavens and earth~~
Rose out of Chaos: ~~or, if Sion hill~~
~~Delight thee more, and Siloa's brook that flowed~~
~~Fast by the oracle of God, I thence~~
~~Invoke thy aid to my adventurous~~ song,
~~That with no middle flight intends to soar~~
~~Above th' Aonian mount, while it pursues~~
~~Things unattempted yet in prose or rhyme.~~

STEPHEN YENSER ON RONALD JOHNSON'S *Radi os*

Paradise Lost—lost, here, anew, these traces tell. We owe them to
Ronald Johnson (1935–1998), who printed them on the first page of his
Radi os. They are the result of his quarrying and sculpting of a page of
Milton's poem, the first thirteen lines of Book I. Working perhaps un-
der the influence of Tom Phillips' project entitled *A Humument* (begun
in 1967), Johnson has whited-out or chipped away the words by Milton
that he did not want. Seeing Johnson's poem partly freed from that mar-
moreal pentameter is rather like seeing one of Michelangelo's captives
emerging from his block of stone. Or we could say that we're seeing the
result of an erosion of those lines, since the force at work has been es-
sentially erotic, a labor of Love, a response in kind to the weathering by
Time of a papyrus fragment of Sappho—whose poem, like any poem,

could only have been *residua* of the poet even when complete. Or that we're reading a transcript of a staticky radio communication over a great distance—from the seventeenth century, say, or from another world, where the ways of God are a possible subject for a poem.

The *radi* that reminds us how much of English has its roots in Latin combines with the *os* that refers to the mouth, and the *os* that signifies bone, to conjure, in a phrase, lyrical relics. What's left of epic unity is runic plurality. Rather than the harmony of the spheres, we have the painstakingly plucked melody. Instead of the totalizing O (the absent because circumfluent center of "G-D"), we have *Os*—in "OS," in "O I" (vowels of primitive lament? digits of binary notation?), in the invocatory "O" (the mouth opened in joy or terror, the egg at the beginning, the word-sliver from Milton that in this fragmentation represents entirety and nullity at once), and in every "line" but two ("Man" and "tree" stand alone): intO, wOrld, chOsen, rOse, Out, Of, chaOs, sOng. Just as Johnson's *trouvaille* makes a little "constellation," to borrow Thibaudet's term for fifteen sequential words in Mallarmé, so its iterated vowel invites us to find within it something like raindrops radiating on a pond.

The first "song" rose out of the silence, the *mise-en-page* implies, as the letters out of the void that is the white sheet (Mallarmé's *vide papier que la blancheur défend*), the "tree" out of chaos or nothing—like the one at the inception of Rilke's *Sonnets to Orpheus* ("*Da stieg ein Baum*"). It is one tree because the Hebraic tree of knowledge and the Christian rood, among others, are branches of the great ash tree, Yggdrasil, the tree of the universe, just as *tree* and *true* are ramifications of the Indo-European *deru,* but it is many because it puts down trunks then roots everywhere, like a banyan (the "fig-tree" that in *Paradise Lost* "spreads her arms, / Branching so broad and long, that on the ground / The bended twigs take root, and daughters grow / About the mother tree").

Radi os was published in Berkeley by Sand Dollar Press in 1977. Prefaced by Johnson's note and dedication and followed by Guy Davenport's afterword, it consists of eighty-four unnumbered pages culled from the first four books of *Paradise Lost.* As far as I know, it has not been reprinted, except for a few pages from its third part that appear in *To Do As Adam Did: Selected Poems of Ronald Johnson* (Talisman House, 2000), edited by Peter O'Leary. Whether it is the overlooked poem that this occasion demands, or this section of it is (for Johnson composed or

de-composed each page with an eye to its integrity), pointless to argue.
Indeed, Johnson might justly observe that the poem overlooked was
Paradise Lost.

[Note: Since I wrote the above paragraphs, *Radi os* has been republished in a handsome edition by Flood Editions. This volume includes the valuable Afterword by Davenport.]

Modifications

RON KOERTGE

When I was young and we were poor and I used to
gripe about the food, my mother would say
"Eat what's in front of you and be thankful you
ain't worse off." That didn't make much of an
impression then and after I left home I didn't
think any more about it except to make fun,
you know how that goes. Then a few months ago
I had a lot of trouble, nothing that most
people couldn't handle but I'm not most people
and it wigged me out all but for good. The
only way I held my junk-shop life together was
by remembering all the good old rules: So now
I honor my father and mother like crazy, go to
bed real early, take hundreds of stitches
in time but most of all I eat what's put in front
of me. Lately I've eaten a lot of forks and
things and right now there's a nice waitress in the
hospital just because she didn't move her hand in
time. It's too bad but I've just got to have the
rules to keep my arms and legs from flying off, so
whenever I sit down I think them over and chew 50
times and say thank you thank you thank you thank
you thank you thank you thank you thank you thank
you thank you thank you thank you thank you.

The summer between my sophomore and junior years at Woon-socket High School, I signed up for a program called Brown Summer High School. I'd just received my license and I felt amazingly grown up in my decade-old yellow Impala. I believe I drove five other kids in that huge car, with room to spare, taking route 146 to Providence, then tak-ing a dozen or so back-and-forth tries in order to satisfactorily parallel park on College Hill. Though only a half-hour away from the house I grew up in, Brown University was as exotic as Tahiti. I was sure the grass there smelled different, i.e., smarter and sweeter. I'd signed up for writ-ing and literature classes, while my friends had signed up for drama.

My favorite class was creative writing, taught by a woman (perhaps, looking back, a young grad student) with a penchant for long feathery earrings and peasant skirts. She played music while we wrote. She had us write responses to pictures on Tarot cards. She was wild and free and encouraging in a way that my high school teachers were not. She made us read our work aloud just minutes after we wrote it, and she also brought in examples by contemporary writers. All of the pieces she showed us were short stories except for Ron Koertge's "Modifications." I don't even remember if our teacher told us this was a poem. But I remember being moved in my gut, completely enraptured. I gave it to my drama student friends to read aloud like a dramatic monologue on the way back to Woonsocket, just to hear how each one would interpret those thirteen unpunctuated thank yous at the end.

I was blown away by the casual chattiness of the poem—"you know how that goes" and "I honor my mother and father like crazy" and the way Koertge's speaker subverted clichés by taking them literally. I kept this poem in my wallet for about a decade, long after college and grad school, until my wallet was stolen. I like to imagine that the thief found Koertge's poem, the blue mimeographed letters insistent on the thin-ning paper, and perhaps it changed his life, too.

When, for my high school senior English class, we all had to mem-orize a poem (or song lyric—since the teacher caved in when many students complained that they hated poetry), I memorized "Modifica-tions." Student after student recited a lyric by Bob Dylan or Van Mor-rison, then I got up and gave a heartfelt rendition of Koertge's "Modifications." Easily bored football players liked it, squeaky pep-squad members liked it, potheads liked it.

They all asked, "Where did you find that thing?" I remember copying out the poem by hand for interested classmates. It appealed to our adolescent angst—we all knew what was ahead was "a lot of trouble" and most of us were terrified of graduating. More than a few of us, hormones raging, felt like we too were on the edge of madness. Yet Koertge's easy distance in the poem, his refusal to take it all too seriously, made "Modifications" safe to be around.

Quick cut twenty or so years. I come across a poet named Ron Koertge—*Making Love to Roget's Wife*—and the name looks so strange to me and at the same time so familiar. I write to him and ask—did you write a poem that ends with thirteen thank yous? I have lost the title with my wallet, I remember something about someone chewing off someone's hand in a mental hospital. Yes, Koertge says, and I beg him for a copy. He writes back, "1977? 1978? I didn't keep my magazines back then. . . ." The poem didn't make it into any of his books. He suggests, "Maybe it was in an early copy of *Wormwood Review*?" Anyway, I search and I search until, one day, I type Koertge's name, followed by "thank you thank you thank you thank you thank you thank you thank you thank you thank you thank you thank you thank you thank you," in Google.com. It's a desperate measure, a desperate longing for this poem that had meant so much to me, and there it is, like some hidden jewel. The poem stings me the same way it did when I first came across it. I e-mail it to Ron, who writes back, "Hmm . . . it's not bad."

Watching TV

JOANNE KYGER

Ahoy!   Electronic nightmare. . . .
         You don't see many Skunks watching TV
       that is,   if you are watching the tube
     you never get to see Skunk outside strolling
      in the full moon toward the compost. Good Evening.
    He lifts his tail. I'm just strolling, so all is well
with the smell.

      A topographical enlightenment is swooning
in the back yard. Look at the sky tonight! View
    the promenade of crisp hedges today. 'The world
      around us is workable' when the mind
     is unfettered and away from the tube, the screen;
    the eyeball engaged in a back lighted room—mind tomb.

Then full moon Skunk appears   delightful
                with tiny frightened screams.

HOA NGUYEN AND DALE SMITH ON JOANNE KYGER'S Watching TV

Joanne Kyger has made her home in the northern California town of Bolinas since the late 1960s; her work is suffused with a sense of that place. Before moving to Bolinas, Joanne lived and traveled in Japan and India with the poet Gary Snyder, with whom she developed a lifelong Zen practice that continues to influence her work. (*Strange Big Moon,* a prose narrative from her notebooks and letters of that time, documents her life with Snyder in Asia, which includes a sojourn to India in the company of Allen Ginsberg.) Part of the San Francisco Renaissance of poets in the 1950s, Joanne frequented North Beach bars with Jack Spicer, Robert Duncan, and others in an apprenticeship of extraordinary depth and energy.

In the '60s and '70s, Bolinas was a hippie arcadia of great dope, wonderful company, alternative lifestyles, and scenic excursions. At one time, Robert Creeley, *Paris Review* editor Tom Clark, *New American Poetry* editor Donald Allen, poet David Meltzer, novelist Richard Brautigan, and many other writers, musicians, and artists lived in the flower-power paradise. Although in recent years the price of Marin County real estate has turned many hippies into yuppies, Bolinas remains an outpost for artists and writers, and Joanne's home continues to be a kind of hearth for visiting poets today.

She once said that Robert Duncan kept "an unabashedly magical house;" this is also true of the home Joanne shares with poet Donald Guravich. Books line the walls. There are exotic treasures from her travels, including Buddhist deities, totemic shrines, and musical instruments, as well as bowls full of agate, jade, and polished glass collected on beach hikes. From her porch or through a window, you might see a family of quail enter the yard cautiously, then feast on seed Joanne has left for them. A visit can reach epic proportions: Local artists stop by for dinner or drinks, listen to recordings, play music, and gossip about poets. "You haven't heard of Jaime de Angulo?" Joanne will ask, thrusting a book into your hands. "Well here, you *must* read his work." A collaborative poem is usually in progress on the typewriter. Joanne reminds participants not to hesitate with the words, just to let them flow.

Her engagement with organic life processes is often mirrored in the construction of her poems on the page, wherein lines are released into the white space rather than stacked along the left-hand margin. "I saw the page as some kind of tapestry and voice glyph," Joanne said in a 1997 interview, echoing poetic concerns that have been with her since her first book, *The Tapestry and the Web.* "The whole movement and rhythm on the page give us instruction as to voice and phrasing and import of what's going on."

"Watching TV," like many of Joanne's poems, exhibits on a first reading a deceptive ease. The form is open, conversational, visually intriguing, composed as if by field—to use the language of Olson's "Projective Verse," an essay that Joanne first encountered in 1957. "Watching TV" also evinces her accuracy of image and language.

The skunk literally leads us into the poem, to the poet's living room. Televised images are vomited as from a worm's mouth against the striking, potentially stinking, image of the little beast, which shakes up Joanne's routine, calling attention to the habit of television, manifesting a surprising form in the dark outdoors. More than just a skunk, the creature is an instance of the cosmic pattern as perceived (with humor) by the poet. It realigns her sense of mission within the mundane domestic blast of TV, opening her eyes to the simple charms of the night sky.

A trusty recorder of daily life, Joanne approaches the quotidian and the sublime via subtle observations. She can sketch a landscape with a few strokes, letting image settle next to image provocatively. In "View North," dedicated to the memory of poet Larry Eigner, she writes: "Back dropped / blue-grey clouds / warm lull / a spot of sun / in this clearing / of moment transferred— / a perfectly peaceful point / of view." Language also is a process of self-inquiry, the poetic field a space for the disruptions and intrusions essential to discovering the unknown content within herself and within the physical or creative environments she inhabits by force. In Joanne's work, the mind, trapped at first within the gridlock of daily routine and social demands, is interrupted; attention is redirected, through the breath of the poem, to the natural world.

Although she has been left out of recent anthologies, Joanne's newly published *As Ever: Selected Poems* presents more than forty years of poetic achievement. She is, as poet and critic Ron Silliman notes, "one of our hidden treasures—the poet who really links the Beats, the Spicer Circle, the Bolinas poets, the New York School, and the language poets, and the only poet who can be said to do all of the above." Beyond such lineages and linkages, Joanne is a religious poet with a demanding intelligence. Language is the medium between her and the world, the poetic field her space for registering diverse occasions in time.

Tortoise Shout

D. H. LAWRENCE

I thought he was dumb,
I said he was dumb,
Yet I've heard him cry.

First faint scream,
Out of life's unfathomable dawn,
Far off, so far, like a madness, under the horizon's dawning rim,
Far, far off, far scream.

Tortoise *in extremis.*

Why were we crucified into sex?
Why were we not left rounded off, and finished in ourselves,
As we began,
As he certainly began, so perfectly alone?

A far, was-it-audible scream,
Or did it sound on the plasm direct?

Worse than the cry of the new-born,
A scream,
A yell,
A shout,
A paean,
A death-agony,
A birth-cry,
A submission,
All tiny, tiny, far away, reptile under the first dawn.

War-cry, triumph, acute-delight, death-scream reptilian,
Why was the veil torn?
The silken shriek of the soul's torn membrane?
The male soul's membrane
Torn with a shriek half music, half horror.

Crucifixion.
Male tortoise, cleaving behind the hovel-wall of that dense female,
Mounted and tense, spread-eagle, out-reaching out of the shell
In tortoise-nakedness,
Long neck, and long vulnerable limbs extruded, spread-eagle over her
    house-roof,
And the deep, secret, all-penetrating tail curved beneath her walls,
Reaching and gripping tense, more reaching anguish in uttermost
    tension
Till suddenly, in the spasm of coition, tupping like a jerking leap, and
    oh!
Opening its clenched face from his outstretched neck
And giving that fragile yell, that scream,
Super-audible,
From his pink, cleft, old-man's mouth,
Giving up the ghost,
Or screaming in Pentecost, receiving the ghost.

His scream, and his moment's subsidence,
The moment of eternal silence,
Yet unreleased, and after the moment, the sudden, startling jerk of
    coition, and at once
The inexpressible faint yell—
And so on, till the last plasm of my body was melted back
To the primeval rudiments of life, and the secret.

So he tups, and screams
Time after time that frail, torn scream
After each jerk, the longish interval,
The tortoise eternity,
Age-long, reptilian persistence,
Heart-throb, slow heart-throb, persistent for the next spasm.

I remember, when I was a boy,
I heard the scream of a frog, which was caught with his foot in the
        mouth of an up-starting snake;
I remember when I first heard bull-frogs break into sound in the
        spring;
I remember hearing a wild goose out of the throat of night
Cry loudly, beyond the lake of waters;
I remember the first time, out of a bush in the darkness, a nightingale's
        piercing cries and gurgles startled the depths of my soul;
I remember the scream of a rabbit as I went through a wood at
        midnight;
I remember the heifer in her heat, blorting and blorting through the
        hours, persistent and irrepressible,
I remember my first terror hearing the howl of weird, amorous cats;
I remember the scream of a terrified, injured horse, the sheet-
        lightning,
And running away from the sound of a woman in labour, something
        like an owl whooing,
And listening inwardly to the first bleat of a lamb,
The first wail of an infant,
And my mother singing to herself,
And the first tenor singing of the passionate throat of a young collier,
        who has long since drunk himself to death,
The first elements of foreign speech
On wild dark lips.

And more than all these,
And less than all these,
This last,
Strange, faint coition yell
Of the male tortoise at extremity,
Tiny from under the very edge of the farthest far-off horizon of life.

The cross,
The wheel on which our silence first is broken,
Sex, which breaks up our integrity, our single inviolability, our deep
    silence,
Tearing a cry from us.

Sex, which breaks us into voice, sets us calling across the deeps, calling,
    calling for the complement,
Singing, and calling, and singing again, being answered, having found.

Torn, to become whole again, after long seeking for what is lost,
The same cry from the tortoise as from Christ, the Osiris-cry of
    abandonment,
That which is whole, torn asunder,
That which is in part, finding its whole again throughout the universe.

DAVID ST. JOHN ON D. H. LAWRENCE'S Tortoise Shout

D. H. Lawrence's power and accomplishment as a poet have always
been undervalued. His fame as a novelist, short-story writer, and essay-
ist has dominated both critical and popular estimations of his work. His
Complete Poems weighs in at 950 pages and, the truth is, much of this
work feels occasional, polemical, and slight. But I also happen to believe
that Lawrence wrote two of the most dazzling and compelling books of
poetry of the first part of the twentieth century: *Look! We Have Come
Through!* and *Birds, Beasts, and Flowers.*

Look! We Have Come Through! was begun in 1912 and finished, as
Lawrence says, "at the end of the bitter winter of 1916–17." It is a se-
quence of love poems charting his and Frieda's flight from England (and
her husband and children) to travel in Europe during the year they
awaited her difficult divorce—a poetic diary of the oscillations of a rela-
tionship. It's also a rehearsal for some of the most compelling elements
we later find in *Women In Love.*

The poem I have chosen is in the Whitmanic, stylistically sprawl-
ing *Birds, Beasts, and Flowers.* In this collection, Lawrence tries to return
to the natural world some of the dignity he feels man has so casually

stripped away, while at the same time looking into the mirror of the natural world, to its cast of animal and botanical life, often to expose the oddness, weakness, and silliness of men. "Tortoise Shout" is the last in a cycle of six poems about tortoises, beginning with "Baby Tortoise" and passing through several poems of, well, let's call it tortoise courtship. "Tortoise Shout" becomes, of course, a poem concerned also with the burden and transcendence of human sexuality. The center passage of the poem, the passage of the liturgical "I remember . . ." details of Lawrence's childhood, is simply electrifying. Discover this poem at your leisure, then go back and read the entire collection. Let me end by saying that, if you admire Galway Kinnell, especially the Kinnell of *The Book of Nightmares,* you should know that the presiding influence (as Kinnell has made clear), other than Rilke, is the poetry of D. H. Lawrence. It's time we all gave Lawrence his poetic due.

In Answer to Your Query

NAOMI LAZARD

We are sorry to inform you
the item you ordered
is no longer being produced.
It has not gone out of style
nor have people lost interest in it.
In fact, it has become
one of our most desired products.
Its popularity is still growing.
Orders for it come in
at an ever increasing rate.
However, a top-level decision
has caused this product
to be discontinued forever.

Instead of the item you ordered
we are sending you something else.
It is not the same thing,
nor is it a reasonable facsimile.
It is what we have in stock,
the very best we can offer.

If you are not happy
with this substitution
let us know as soon as possible.
As you can imagine
we already have quite an accumulation
of letters such as the one
you may or may not write.
To be totally fair
we respond to these complaints
as they come in.
Yours will be filed accordingly,
answered in its turn.

CAROLYN KIZER ON NAOMI LAZARD'S In Answer to Your Query

All too frequently in our household, we experience what we have come to call a "Naomi Moment." It occurs when a product or a service that we have counted on ceases to exist: collar stays, a grilled chicken sandwich, a certain shade of lipstick, pool equipment parts, and items from L. L. Bean. These big and little frustrations are summed up, with only a trace of hyperbole, in Naomi Lazard's "In Answer to Your Query."

Twenty-five years ago, the poems in her book *Ordinances* had won prizes and great acclaim. It's not hard to see why. With unerring accuracy Ms. Lazard skewered the varied voices of bureaucracies in our consumerist society. It's a voice eerily like the automated one we get when we phone our bank or the airlines or the telephone company itself. "In Answer to Your Query" begins: "We are sorry to inform you / the item you ordered / is no longer being produced. / It has not gone out of style

. . . in fact, it has become / one of our most desired products . . . However, a top-level decision / has caused this product / to be discontinued forever." The reader receives the message with a chuckle and a groan: Ah satire! Ah stringent social commentary! How rare they are.

So why has this splendid poem, and its sisters, dropped from sight? Because this is the last book that Lazard has published. But these poems should not be allowed to be forgotten. They are truer than ever today— in fact, we could suggest some additional topics that need to come under her basilisk gaze. Won't someone please reprint *Ordinances?* I know at least fifteen major poets who would leap at the chance to introduce it.

The Morning After My Death

LARRY LEVIS

I.

My body is a white thing in the sun, now.
It is not ashamed of itself,
Not anymore. Because today is
The morning after my death.
How little I have to say;
How little desire I have
To say it.

And these flies sleeping on doorsills
And hugging screens; and the child
Who has just run out of the house
After touching my body, who knows,
Suddenly, how heavy a dead man is . . .

What can the sun do but keep shining?
Even though I don't especially need it
Anymore, it shines on the palm fronds
And makes them look older,

The way someone who writes a letter,
And then tears it up, looks suddenly older.

2.

Far off, a band is playing Sousa marches.
And as the conductor, in his sun stained
Uniform, taps his baton for silence, and all
Around him the foliage is getting greener,
Greener, like the end of things,
One of the musicians, resting
His trumpet on his knee, looks around
A moment, before he spits and puts the horn
Into his mouth, counting slowly.

And so I think of the darkness inside the horn,
How no one's breath has been able
To push it out yet, into the air,
How when the concert ends it will still
Be there, like a note so high no one
Can play it, or like the dried blood inside
A dead woman's throat, when the mourners
Listen, and there is nothing left but these flies,
Polished and swarming frankly in the sun.

CHRISTOPHER BUCKLEY ON LARRY LEVIS'
The Morning After My Death

Larry Levis received book prizes, NEA grants, Guggenheim and Fulbright fellowships, yet as one of the most important and original poets of the last thirty years, he was overlooked. For no reason, I suppose, beyond the usual politics of poetry, his work was not included in the Norton anthology or in Poulin's Houghton Mifflin *Contemporary Poetry*. The University of Pittsburgh Press, most recently with *The Selected Levis* (2002), is keeping his recent books in print, and Carnegie Mellon University Press has reprinted two earlier books.

In general, Levis' second book, *The Afterlife* (1977), which contains "The Morning After My Death," has been overlooked. However, there are poems in this book unlike anything else anyone was writing in the mid-1970s, poems that would define the range and originality of Larry's voice and vision. While many of the poems in *The Afterlife* were still in the deep image/semi-surrealist Iowa Writers' Workshop mode, the most impressive and original work—"Rhododendrons," "The Double," the long concluding poem "Linnets," and "The Morning After My Death"—speak in a voice that takes a quantum leap forward in lyric poetry. This voice is clear, direct, modest, emotionally engaging, and objective at the same time; it is also inventive and imaginative. These poems are the first in that voice readers will come to know in subsequent books as Larry's, and only Larry's.

Unfortunately, *The Selected Levis* omits "The Morning After My Death." With this poem and the others mentioned above, Larry invents his own rhetoric of the imagination that allows the vision to go further, the scene and its emotional impact to include more. His logic and concentration in the vignette fix the reader deep inside the poem and its moment in time; the vision of the poem is intensified by such specificity and intense focus. The voice—wistful, resigned, clipped as if adding yet one more remembered detail or inevitability—gives us a tone, a credible texture of pathos. The rhythm of resignation in the lines, in their declaration, in their unassuming epiphanies, and in their detailed imagination, ring with authenticity. The emotional truth, the conceptual truth of such a point in time, of this scenario, comes forward to compel readers emotionally and propel them through the experience/conceit Levis is holding up to the light. In the speaker's mortality, he has an empathy for all of us—the child running out of the house, the dead woman at the end of the poem.

"The Morning After My Death" begins, as we should surmise from the title, with the spirit speaking, but what he has to say has relevance for those who are determined to "have their say," those, perhaps, who place career above all else: "How little I have to say; / How little desire I have / To say it." There is no complaint, no self-pity, but rather a wholly new take on this experience in which the speaker is resigned, washed clean of ambition, objective, interested, observant. With this book, and particularly in this poem, Levis looks consistently into the metaphysical, but on a continuum that is largely secular and mundane—there is not all that much, it seems, beyond this.

The second section of the poem moves to the tactless and middle-brow plane of the world marching on—to Sousa, no less. This is where the imagination enters with the attendant irony and secular darkness and the flat facts of death, and the small life that feeds off it. One of Larry's main gifts was his intense and specific imagination, his power to conceptualize and go out into the realms of invention and possibility and connect them to an accessible and experiential base, an emotional human event that convinced readers that he knew it firsthand. Isn't it then the frankness of the presentation here that makes the imaginative leap into the darkness inside the horn so credible, so matter-of-fact—that musician spitting, counting slowly to begin to play?

Some might think it pretentious for a young poet to title his second book "The Afterlife." Yet the honesty, power, and freshness of the voice sustain the vision, and no conceit is more risky than this one. Larry had the talent, the gift, beginning with this poem to be bold and believable and, in the depth of his introspection, compelling as well. This poem offers us what might surface after wrestling with great doubt and old great fears—the poet's acceptance of some clear space that will let him speak about the small space in the world that he has carved out with his attention, love, and imagination. As it concludes with the factual detail of the flies, they are "polished" and "swarming frankly in the sun" and so, for my reading, are a simple image of life, any life, valued beyond death. The voice in this poem is given wholly to living, an almost Zen appreciation of life, and every daily contradiction of that fact.

Three Moves

JOHN LOGAN

Three moves in six months and I remain
the same.
Two homes made two friends.
The third leaves me with myself again.
(We hardly speak.)
Here I am with tame ducks
and my neighbors' boats,
only this electric heat
against the April damp.
I have a friend named Frank—
the only one who ever dares to call
and ask me, "How's your soul?"
I hadn't thought about it for a while,
and was ashamed to say I didn't know.
I have no priest for now.
Who
will forgive me then. Will you?
Tame birds and my neighbors' boats.
The ducks honk about the floats . . .
They walk dead drunk onto the land and grounds,
iridescent blue and black and green and brown.
They live on swill
our aged houseboats spill.
But still they are beautiful.
Look! The duck with its unlikely beak
has stopped to pick
and pull
at the potted daffodil.
Then again they sway home
to dream
bright gardens of fish in the early night.
Oh these ducks are all right.
They will survive.
But I am sorry I do not often see them climb.

Poor sons-a-bitching ducks.
You're all fucked up.
What do you do that for?
Why don't you hover near the sun anymore?
Afraid you'll melt?
These foolish ducks lack a sense of guilt,
and so all their multi-thousand-mile range
is too short for the hope of change.

LUCIA PERILLO ON JOHN LOGAN'S Three Moves

Because John Logan's was one of the first poetry readings I attended, it became a yardstick of sorts. And because "Three Moves" was always the cornerstone of his readings, the poem has claimed a spot in my psyche as archetype for what a poem should do and be.

What I remember is a frail and balding fair-haired man who read the poem in a high and reedy voice. His intonations reminded me of Chinese speakers: he gave the syllables of the poem (and note how many of its words are monosyllabic) a specific and varying pitch. Though the poem would have been almost twenty years old by then, he spoke it as though it continued to startle him, as though he hadn't encountered it in a long while or had just written it. "Poor sons-a-bitching ducks": Logan's voice was warbling and breathy. He also must have had a new and ill-fitting set of dentures, which added a clacking syncopation to his delivery. He reminded me of a duck.

I've always been a tad afraid that my enthusiasm for this poem springs from the fact that my first hearing of it was an inaugurating moment in my life as a poet. But, as always when I revisit this poem, I am amazed. Only from Emily Dickinson's poetry will a reader get better schooling in the use of rhyme.

About twenty years after the poem was written (in 1965), the debate would heat up between the self-proclaimed "New Formalists" and the run-of-the-mill poets whose default mode of composition was free verse. The importance of "Three Moves" lies in how slyly it puts this debate to rest. As in Hitchcock's movie *Rope,* the poem performs the trick of hiding an obvious thing by putting it in plain view. Call/soul/while.

Now/know. I must have read "Three Moves" dozens of times before I even realized that it *did* rhyme.

The poem makes clear that setting free verse in opposition to formal poetry is wasted energy. It also shows the lie in much of our conventional wisdom: rhyme is dull and retrograde, rhyme circumscribes a poem's emotional range. Or conversely, that we need free verse to write genuine poems of plain speech.

Logan was a contemporary of the poets James Wright, Robert Bly, and Richard Hugo, and like these men he possesses a sensibility whose overblown romantic nature is part of what gives his poetry its grandeur. Logan is arguably the most wistful of this gang, perhaps because of his poems' geographical uprootedness, which "Three Moves" specifically takes on as its subject. Ever the transplant, Logan often dated his poems and listed the places where they were composed. He is the perpetual exile, latching onto whatever constant his environment supplies him with only to find that the constant is in fact unstable: the ducks are all fucked up.

My favorite pairing in the poem is the rhyming of *guilt* and *melt:* in these lines I hear Logan's Chinese-y voice, rising once more like a duck on the wing.

Aftermath

HENRY WADSWORTH LONGFELLOW

When the summer fields are mown,
When the birds are fledged and flown,
And the dry leaves strew the path;
With the falling of the snow,
With the cawing of the crow,
Once again the fields we mow
And gather in the aftermath.

Not the sweet, new grass with flowers
Is this harvesting of ours;
Not the upland clover bloom;
But the rowen mixed with weeds,
Tangled tufts from marsh and meads,
Where the poppy drops its seeds
In the silence and the gloom.

JOHN HOLLANDER ON HENRY WADSWORTH LONGFELLOW'S Aftermath

In choosing an overlooked poem to take a new look at, I had thought of presenting Dante Gabriel Rossetti's strange sonnet "A Match with the Moon." Or possibly Jean Ingelow's surprising poem "Failure." But since I have written on both of these elsewhere, I decided on a very short poem by Henry Wadsworth Longfellow, a poet once over- and long since underpraised (the mandates of Modernism had shaped, particularly for my generation, knowledgeable readers' expectations for poetry). But even the secondary kind of acquaintance with Longfellow's poems that later twentieth-century literary experience would espouse—knowing the names and a line or two from what had become celebrated as antipoetic literary chestnuts—would be limited to *The Song of Hiawatha,* "Evangeline," "The Village Blacksmith," "The Wreck of the Hesperus," and, of course, "Paul Revere's Ride." More knowledgeable readers of poetry might adduce fine, strong poems like "The Fire of Drift-Wood," "The Bells of San Blas," "My Lost Youth," "Mezzo

Cammin," "The Cross of Snow," "The Tide Rises, the Tide Falls," and "Kéramos" as evidence of Longfellow's stature. But with the exception of Richard Wilbur and Howard Nemerov, critical attention has not focused on "Aftermath."

This little work appeared as the title poem of a volume published in 1873, which contained the third part of Longfellow's long sequence called *Tales of a Wayside Inn*—a sort of minor *Canterbury Tales* of which the first one, told by the innkeeper and called "Paul Revere's Ride," is the most famous. The 1873 book also included the final "flight"—or section—of a sequence of shorter poems called "Birds of Passage." The *Tales of a Wayside Inn* were completed on Longfellow's sixty-sixth birthday, and this may be of some relevance as well. The title, "Aftermath," at first invokes our common use of the word today: a consequence or result of something (and most often, that something and its result being unfortunate, or even catastrophic). But the word originally meant after-math (the Old English *math* being cognate with *mow* and *meadow*): a second, or later mowing, the crop of grass that springs up after the mowing in early summer. It is almost synonymous with the word "rowen," used in the second stanza, which means a second crop, perhaps of hay, in a season (it comes from the older French *regain,* cognate with our *regain,* coming from the same French word; and Longfellow may well have known this and allowed for its significance). The figurative "aftermath"—of consequences rather than grasses—is common in the literature of the last half of the nineteenth century. The first two stanzas of Emily Dickinson's "The murmuring of bees has ceased; / But murmuring of some / Posterior, prophetic, / Has simultaneous come" (Johnson #1115) were published as a poem by Dickinson's friend Mabel Loomis Todd in her 1896 edition, with the added title "Aftermath," which changes the figurative focus of the word slightly but still feels grossly irrelevant. Todd may have known Longfellow's poem.

But here *aftermath* is literal, not figurative, even as Longfellow had used it earlier in *Giles Crey of the Salem Farms,* Act III (one of *The New England Tragedies*), where the farmer Corey announces: "We are going to mow / The Ipswich meadows for the aftermath, / The crop of sedge and rowens." And despite the general use of *aftermath* in the figurative sense in nineteenth-century literature, Longfellow keeps to the original one here; this is a georgic poem (rather than a pastoral one) in the highest sense, concentrating on specific agricultural activity. It allegorizes subtly though strongly, rather than manifestly preaching, and seems in some ways a precursor to Robert Frost's wonderful early "Mowing." What it doesn't do is precisely what makes it so distinguished, if obscure, a Longfellow poem. All too often, the modern sensibility, mindful of this poet's great gifts, recoils in disappointment and distaste from his apparent need to pound out the obvious. Longfellow almost ruins his beautiful "Snow-Flakes," for example, with a plodding central stanza in which he orates an explicit analogy that will be beautifully insinuated in the final stanza:

> This is the poem of the air,
>> Slowly in silent syllables recorded;
> This is the secret of despair,
>> Long in its cloudy bosom hoarded,
>>> Now whispered and revealed
>>> In wood and field.

But there is no such moralizing in "Aftermath." This somber, realistic, autumnal lyric deploys the figurative *aftermath* only by deep implication, even as its meditative power emerges from the concrete, present facts themselves. The allegorical extensions of the late mowing go past the conventional topic of "sowing (x) only to reap (y)" into a later stage of consequentiality and, more generally, into matters of age and lateness and the completion of tasks. The final detail of the poppy ushering in darkness and night barely invokes that plant's narcotic powers as it closes down the whole poem. In its own way, "Aftermath" quietly manifests William Carlos Williams' celebrated but more loudly proclaimed "no ideas but in things" of over a half-century later.

The Garden by Moonlight

AMY LOWELL

A black cat among roses,
Phlox, lilac-misted under a first-quarter moon,
The sweet smells of heliotrope and night-scented stock.
The garden is very still,
It is dazed with moonlight,
Contented with perfume,
Dreaming the opium dreams of its folded poppies.
Firefly lights open and vanish
High as the tip buds of the golden glow
Low as the sweet alyssum flowers at my feet.
Moon-shimmer on leaves and trellises,
Moon-spikes shafting through the snow ball bush.
Only the little faces of the ladies' delight are alert and staring,
Only the cat, padding between the roses,
Shakes a branch and breaks the chequered pattern
As water is broken by the falling of a leaf.
Then you come,
And you are quiet like the garden,
And white like the alyssum flowers,
And beautiful as the silent sparks of the fireflies.
Ah, Beloved, do you see those orange lilies?
They knew my mother,
But who belonging to me will they know
When I am gone.

D. A. POWELL ON AMY LOWELL'S The Garden by Moonlight

When I first began reading the Modernists, Amy Lowell had already become little more than a footnote to the work of Ezra Pound. His insistence that she had ruined his early movement, Imagism, seemed entirely justified by the one Amy Lowell poem that was repeatedly anthologized, the awful "Patterns." But when I read her transgressively erotic poem "Venus Transiens" in the newly published *Norton Anthology of*

Literature by Women, I began to suspect that Pound had been wrong. It seemed plausible to me, knowing what I knew of E. P. by then, that he was perhaps jealous of Lowell's work and Lowell's seemingly larger audience. Perhaps his dismissal had more to do with ego than with craft.

Indeed, as I read more and more of Amy Lowell's brand of Imagism, I began to see that in fact she was an artful practitioner of Modernist tendencies, drawing upon the same deft strokes in Chinese and Japanese poetries that Pound had mined. Moreover, Lowell was creating an eroticized world in which her relationship with Ada Russell was central, pushing the boundaries of gender, sexuality, and social mores. Whereas Stein employed code words for her lesbianism in writing about her relationship with Alice Toklas, Lowell was drawing upon the natural world—in the way that Whitman had done in his homoerotic "Calamus" poems—to write lyrical, openly sexual love poems to Russell.

Oddly, Pound's dismissal of Lowell has remained canonical, without anyone really challenging the heterosexism and misogyny that might have been behind it. Too bad, because I think contemporary readers would find great pleasure in Lowell's work, particularly the later poems. This is why I've chosen "The Garden by Moonlight" from Lowell's oeuvre, to showcase her deft use of image and the freshness of tone and diction that shape her work. In this poem, the feminine eros is invoked through the topoi of cat, moonlight, folded poppies, ladies' delight . . . the garden is a metonym of the female body, reminiscent at times of *The Song of Songs.* The yonic energy of the poem culminates in orgasm, described as the sparks of fireflies. And in a moment deeply contemporary, the poet turns at the end to the subject of childlessness, just as the language itself changes from dense, rich texture to a kind of barren tone.

Robert Lowell, writing to Elizabeth Bishop in the 1950s, reports a conversation with Robert Frost, in which the latter Robert said of the former Robert's distant cousin, "somebody really ought to unbury Amy." Since the time I first proposed to include Amy in *Dark Horses,* a new *Selected Poems of Amy Lowell* has appeared, lovingly edited by Melissa Bradshaw and Adrienne Munich. Munich writes that Lowell's "brand of imagism swept away self-consciously poetic diction in favor of a clean, unadorned, musical line." And now Honor Moore has produced a graceful *Selected Poems* of Lowell for the American Poets Project. In the end,

Amy Lowell did indeed fulfill Pound's vision, whether Pound approved of it or not. And Lowell has finally made it into that most hallowed of texts, *The Norton Anthology of Modern Poetry in English.*

Perhaps this is but the beginning of a resurgence of interest in Lowell, as we've had with Mina Loy and with Lorine Niedecker. I hope that more of Lowell's "brand of imagism" will surface, and that the poems will be taught alongside those of her male counterparts. I find in Lowell a grace and daring beyond measure. The pared-down rhythms and the rich imagery of her work are exquisite.

Meeting Point

LOUIS MACNEICE

Time was away and somewhere else,
There were two glasses and two chairs
And two people with the one pulse
(Somebody stopped the moving stairs):
Time was away and somewhere else.

And they were neither up nor down;
The stream's music did not stop
Flowing through heather, limpid brown,
Although they sat in a coffee shop
And they were neither up nor down.

The bell was silent in the air
Holding its inverted poise—
Between the clang and clang a flower,
A brazen calyx of no noise:
The bell was silent in the air.

The camels crossed the miles of sand
That stretched around the cups and plates;
The desert was their own, they planned
To portion out the stars and dates:
The camels crossed the miles of sand.

Time was away and somewhere else.
The waiter did not come, the clock
Forgot them and the radio waltz
Came out like water from a rock:
Time was away and somewhere else.

Her fingers flicked away the ash
That bloomed again in tropic trees:
Not caring if the markets crash
When they had forests such as these,
Her fingers flicked away the ash.

God or whatever means the Good
Be praised that time can stop like this,
That what the heart has understood
Can verify in the body's peace
God or whatever means the Good.

Time was away and she was here
And life no longer what it was,
The bell was silent in the air
And all the room one glow because
Time was away and she was here.

ELISE PASCHEN ON LOUIS MACNEICE'S Meeting Point

 I first encountered the work of Louis MacNeice at graduate school in England, while studying the poetry of W. H. Auden and researching my dissertation on W. B. Yeats. At that time, my colleague and friend, the Irish poet Peter McDonald, also was writing his dissertation on

MacNeice. In *Louis MacNeice: The Poet in His Contexts,* McDonald describes the challenges MacNeice faced: "a 1930s poet who insisted on his Irishness; an Irish-born poet who lived most of his life in England." MacNeice stood and still stands in the shadows of his contemporary, W. H. Auden, as well as his Irish predecessor, Yeats.

Even then, I was aware of the Atlantic divide between the English and American poetry worlds. Most people in Britain didn't read American poets, and most people in the U.S. didn't read British poets. MacNeice, like so many British poets, remained almost totally unknown here.

His books are surprisingly difficult to locate in Chicago, where I now live. While editing a recent poetry anthology, I attempted to track down MacNeice's work at the central public library. No books were to be found. Fortunately, though, I did discover several MacNeice first editions at The Newberry Library, including *The Last Ditch,* published in Dublin in 1940 by Yeats's sisters, Lily and Lollie, who ran Cuala Press. "Meeting Point" arrested my attention then and continues to haunt me with its emotional heart-thrust and incantatory form.

Louis MacNeice wrote "Meeting Point" in April 1939, on the brink of World War II, soon after he completed his acclaimed "Autumn Journal." A single father (his wife, Mary Ezra, had left him and their son, Daniel, in 1935, after five years of marriage, when Dan was a year and a half old), MacNeice had dabbled in various love affairs before experiencing a *coup de foudre* upon meeting the American short-story writer Eleanor Clark in New York City. A Classics professor at London University, he was on an American lecture tour arranged by his Faber & Faber editor, T. S. Eliot. Several weeks after that encounter, on board the *Queen Mary,* headed back to England, he wrote Eleanor a twenty-eight-page letter declaring his love and enclosed the poem "Meeting Point."

In our anthology, *Poetry Speaks,* Rebekah Presson Mosby and I included an audio version of "Meeting Point," which MacNeice recorded at Yale in the early '60s. MacNeice's reading style is polished; for twenty years he worked for the BBC as a broadcaster and scriptwriter. At the beginning of that recording, MacNeice explains the genesis of "Meeting Point": "It's the old idea when two people are very much in love that, wherever they are, they seem in a closed, magic circle of their own. Time, in fact, has stopped, and on the place they're actually in they superimpose their own (so to speak) private landscapes."

"Meeting Point" consists of eight five-line stanzas written in iambic tetrameter, with an *ababa* rhyme scheme. MacNeice frames each stanza with a refrain, freezing the epiphany, as time stops. He encases a moment of "timeless happiness" in the elaborate architecture of his poem. Time transfixed recalls Eliot's "still point of the turning world," but MacNeice published "Meeting Point" before his editor's "Burnt Norton" appeared in 1941.

In "Meeting Point," MacNeice layers his language, his imagery, and the multiple universes of the poem. The "private landscapes" invented by the lovers are contrasted with the stark environment of the coffee shop embodied in the waiter, the clock, and the radio. A surreal world of nature enters the poem in stanza two: the stream's music continues to flow through heather, and in stanza three, the bell (by turning upside down) blossoms into a flower. The natural world arrests time, or the ringing of the bell.

This imaginary landscape culminates in stanza four, where the other world comes to life on the café table: "The camels crossed the miles of sand / That stretched around the cups and plates; / The desert was their own, they planned / To portion out the stars and dates: / The camels crossed the miles of sand." And MacNeice takes the leap in stanza six, where the ash from her cigarette does not land in an ashtray but rather "[blooms] again in tropic trees." To underscore that "unity of being" experienced by the two lovers (though their affair had not been consummated), MacNeice revised the penultimate line from "a glow" in the 1940 edition to "one glow" in the *Collected Poems,* an image that reflects back to stanza one: "one pulse" set against "two people," "two glasses," "two chairs."

MacNeice dedicated *The Last Ditch* to Eleanor Clark and included this epigraph: "Without heroics, without belief, / I send you, as I am not rich, / Nothing but odds and ends a thief / Bundled up in the last ditch." "Meeting Point" was the first love poem he wrote to Eleanor, yet he placed it in the middle of the book, after the sequence "The Coming of War," demonstrating how the artistic sensibility reconfigures the passage of time. The closing stanza in section II in "The Coming of War"—"But, if I am going to be dead / Within a year, / There is someone I should like / Beside me in this bed / And God damn Hitler / That

she is not here"—presages the concluding refrain of "Meeting Point":
"Time was away and she was here."

The placement of "Meeting Point" in the book proves an immutable testament to the power of love, overcoming time and war and geographic divide. When *The Last Ditch* appeared in print, their trans-Atlantic liaison was on the brink of ending. Soon after, MacNeice met and married cabaret singer Hedli Anderson in London. But the immutability of "Meeting Point" transcends the fragility of human relationship.

The Landscape Is Behind the Door

PIERRE MARTORY

TRANSLATED BY JOHN ASHBERY

The landscape is behind the door.
The person is there—New York is full
Of similar places where a world,
A large cloud, is being built. Only
The heads stay put. You pay
Before arriving, a long time before
Opening your mouth. There are things
Near us which all have their green sides.

You wear your eyes and lose them.
A caterpillar makes the difference.
The girl whose face is full of blood
Stops and asks the time.
It's a year that doesn't know its number.
A smile at the bottom of a pocket.
Look! the liar-bird, brother of secrets,
Leaves the familiar creek bed:
The life of others painted on a lampshade.

"I draw you like a salary.
You are my superfluous statue
Hatched beneath hot tears.
I'm digging toward the antipodes,
I unwind the bandages, the horoscope:
It's my body, it's my cocoon, surprised
In a sleep of prolific sand,
That I'm uncovering, like a Cyclops that fainted."

It would be enough to enter, to sit
Near a book, to fold the shadow
To one's knees, to know who
Walks on the bed, who passes the mirror.
Dust tints the linens gray.
Photos choke on night.
Now nothing is visible in the room
Except the inaccessible landscape outdoors.

Down there, the fires of prehistory continue stubbornly
To glow. The lost felucca ferries a skeleton
To its grave. A disc feeds the sky.
In hollows of geysers dolphins are taking
Advantage of their incognito to cry.
A pious hand is strangling the pity
And slips into the letter-box
The perfumed sadness of silence.

The door placarded with such moments
Doesn't open. The cigarettes unrolled
In smoke (a supplementary beauty)
Leave on the fingers the smell of time past.
The distance from inside to outside.
Everything is in place, nothing is missing.
Weary of strife the bee on
The windowpane finally renounces the flower.

The Landscape Is Behind the Door

When I first heard the title of Pierre Martory's collection *The Landscape is Behind the Door,* I felt an instant recognition and a great desire to get my hands on the book and hole up in secret to read it. That most suggestive title assured me there would be secrets revealed and adventures aplenty. Of course, behind some doors there are landscapes of the denotative kind; surely there is enough room behind any door for a landscape of the imagination.

That title, and Martory's poems in general, offer the same pleasure as being taken to see something someone else wants to take you to see—high ledges up in the hills where almost nobody goes, say, or an extraordinary example of radial symmetry in an otherwise ordinary building. (It's also why a book that has been given to you by someone you love or admire can have such delicious, added layers of mystery because of its provenance.) I'm intrigued with the title's assertive sentence and its implied intimacy of address. And I love its resonating openness.

It didn't take long before I found the book and the room to read it in. (It had to be a room with as many doors as a room can have and still qualify as a room; I closed all of them save one, and left that one slightly ajar.) Pierre Martory's poems—thirty-eight of them, a 111–page selection in French and English, translations by John Ashbery, published in 1994 by The Sheep Meadow Press—have such English titles as "What I Say Perhaps, Isn't True," "Undecipherable Archive," "Urb," "Every Question But One," and "A Night on the Dead Sea." The titles themselves beckon: more doors.

Martory's voice is haunted with sadness and unbreakable silences, with grieving of a kind that has no stages. It reaches through the barriers of language with an urgent and tender appeal. One reads these poems as if Martory were at your side reading them with you: his point of view is that palpable, that intimate. A poem begins "Now the moon is too low / For us to leave," and one senses a deeply felt and seriously understood fatality of a passage of time. Another opens thus: "How do you say Tomorrow in this country?" and one wishes for words not yet invented with which to answer his question. "I hang around silence," he says in the beautifully realized longish poem "Toten Insel," and one can hear oneself saying "yes, don't we all"—so we might as well hang around together, one ends up thinking, because Martory's companionship is so welcoming.

John Ashbery, in his introduction to the book, admits no certain knowledge of Martory's influences but gathers a rich array of possible ancestors including Emily Dickinson, Gertrude Stein, Raymond Roussell, Trakl, Hölderlin, and René Char, among others. He gives us a brief and provocative biographical sketch that makes one wish for a full biography. Martory did not seek publication for his poetry in France; his one published novel, *Phebus ou le beau Mariage,* was not followed by any others. Perhaps we have friendship to thank for our seeing these poems in English. John Ashbery and Pierre Martory's friendship dates from 1956. It appears from the introduction that Martory allowed *The Landscape is Behind the Door* to come into print only reluctantly.

"It would be enough to enter, to sit / Near a book, to fold the shadow," he says a few stanzas into "The Landscape is Behind the Door." Martory's poems have many subjects, many nuances of tone, many keys ("I was trying desperately to think of something / That had never occurred to me before"). Sometimes it seems as if he is one of the rarest of a rare sort, one who takes everything and everyone grievously seriously—himself excepted: that is his modesty, ever present in his poems.

The Trees Are Down

CHARLOTTE MEW

> And he cried with a loud voice:
> Hurt not the earth, neither the sea,
> nor the trees
> —Revelation

They are cutting down the great plane-trees at the end of the gardens.
For days there has been the grate of the saw, the swish of the branches
    as they fall,
The crash of trunks, the rustle of trodden leaves,
With the 'Whoops' and the 'Whoas,' the loud common talk, the loud
    common laughs of the men, above it all.

I remember one evening of a long past Spring
Turning in at a gate, getting out of a cart, and finding a large dead rat
    in the mud of the drive.
I remember thinking: alive or dead, a rat was a god-forsaken thing,
But at least, in May, that even a rat should be alive.

The week's work here is as good as done. There is just one bough
    On the roped bole, in the fine grey rain,
        Green and high
        And lonely against the sky.
            (Down now!—)
        And but for that,
        If an old dead rat
Did once, for a moment, unmake the Spring, I might never have
    thought of him again.

It is not for a moment the Spring is unmade to-day;
These were great trees, it was in them from root to stem:
When the men with the 'Whoops' and the 'Whoas' have carted the
      whole of the whispering loveliness away
Half the Spring, for me, will have gone with them.
It is going now, and my heart has been struck with the hearts of the
      planes;
Half my life it has beat with these, in the sun, in the rains,
    In the March wind, the May breeze,
In the great gales that came over to them across the roofs from the
      great seas.
    There was only a quiet rain when they were dying;
    They must have heard the sparrows flying,
And the small creeping creatures in the earth where they were lying—
    But I, all day, I heard an angel crying:
        'Hurt not the trees.'

MOLLY PEACOCK ON CHARLOTTE MEW'S The Trees Are Down

Once I had to get along with some people who could never agree
on anything. Then our neighbor cut down a tree. Instantly we united in
mourning. It is irresistible to identify with trees. Tall emblems of endur-
ance, they possess the special allure of being alive but not animate. They
stay as still as monarchs on their thrones, existing at so perfect a distance
from us that they create a mythic parallel with our human lives.

So humans suffer when we see people cutting down trees, even if
it's for the trees' "own good." And we suffer with outrage if we see no
reason for the felling. To weather a hurricane and still raise your arms in
praise of existence—that is tree-valor.

"The Trees Are Down," with its epigraph from the Book of Rev-
elation, depicts British poet Charlotte Mew's own ideas of valor, and
it might even foreshadow her own end. With her lanky-lined poem,
daring in its combination of near-prosiness with the chant of childlike
rhyme, Mew is the foremother of our current style of lyrical narration,
or narrative lyric. I personally love this poem because of the "swish" and

the "crash" and the "rustle" of the felling and because of the shocking (and everlasting) image of the rat. Mew is utterly conversational but completely rhythmical when she says, "I remember thinking: alive or dead, a rat was a god-forsaken thing, / But at least, in May, that even a rat should be alive." She allows us to enter her consciousness, to share with her the horror at the destruction of the "great plane trees at the end of the gardens," and she is even bold enough to invite us to hear the angel of Revelation at the end. Her poem is protean and alive—treelike in its look and in its long-limbed construction. I wonder, leaving aside obvious reasons of sexism, if perhaps her work nearly disappeared because she created our mode of lyric narration a century too early.

Writing most of her poems from the late 1890s to 1913, Mew published only one book in her lifetime, *The Farmer's Bride,* which was extravagantly praised by Thomas Hardy, Virginia Woolf, Siegfried Sassoon, and Edith Sitwell. Sassoon compared her to Christina Rossetti; Woolf called her "the greatest living poetess"; and Hardy wrote, "Miss Mew is far and away the best living woman poet—who will be read when others are forgotten." Ironically, Mew is so utterly forgotten that you can't even buy her *Complete Poems* in the U.S. (although it is available in England and Canada, published by Penguin).

Mew (1869–1928) was born into a once well-to-do family of architects. Her father lost the family fortune and died, leaving her mother, a beloved sister, and two mentally ill siblings for whom institutional upkeep had to be paid. Mew and her sister vowed never to marry for fear of passing on this illness, though perhaps the stronger reason was Mew's attachment to women. (If you want to visualize her, dress her in what she typically wore: a porkpie hat, tweed topcoat, and boots. Doesn't that look a little like a tree?)

And like those trees in her poems, she too was cut down, but by her own hand. After her mother's death, and after her sister's death, despite the fact that Hardy and Walter de la Mare secured her a pension, she took her own life, dying horribly by drinking a bottle of lye. Once you know this awful fact, it hangs over the work, something to be adjusted to, or gotten rid of, or, perhaps, read through. Even with its images of death, this vigorous poem must have been written at the height of her energy, its lines running like "the great gales that came" "across the roofs from the great seas" in a spirit of outrage and shocked sympathy. It is a testament to a spirited sensuousness that keeps her work vitally alive, and whispering to us, despite our ignorance of her.

I am indebted to John Newton's preface to the *Complete Poems* of Charlotte Mew and to the *Norton Anthology of Literature by Women* for the biographical information about the poet.

The Drive

BERT MEYERS

Because their bed was calm
and they'd never done
what they read about,
they drove to the hills,
left the car, and climbed
high over the shale
and spread her dress in the dirt.

Soft ceramic quail,
the natives there,
stared from the chaparral
while they groaned
and hurt themselves.
The heat made ants
bubble out of the ground.

The hill was a flower
that evening closed.
They were naked
and very small,
and they put on their clothes.
The car would give them back
their power.

I knew instantly, when asked to choose a poem for this anthology, that I must pick a poem, any poem, by Bert Meyers. He is one of the best-kept secrets in Western literature. His name and work are always accompanied in my thoughts by alternating currents of pleasure and sorrow. Pleasure, because his beautifully crafted poems set a lofty example in their precision, deceptive simplicity, wit, exemplary imagery, and tender gravity. Sadness because Meyers died far too young, at fifty-one, of lung cancer, in 1979. Had he lived longer, I believe appreciation for his work would have spread, and there would be no need for him to be recognized now in a collection of neglected poems. Meyers' work has been out of print for decades. His *In a Dybbyk's Raincoat, Collected Poems: 1947–1979* was scheduled to be published by Creative Arts Books, in Berkeley, California, in 2004, but that press went out of business before they could publish it.

I've picked one poem to be reprinted here, but the choice is arbitrary. All Meyers' poems are incredibly resonant and compact. All contain a kind of contemplative, lucid fury and a vibrating religiosity about small moments of peak perception "Here, on this jewel of earth." The voice in the poems is clear and pure, peppered with ethical skepticism. The work combines strength and delicacy, and an elegiac quality with a vigorous appetite for life. Denise Levertov, who wrote an essay on his work, called him "one of the best poets of our time," and commented, "I feel Meyers can be called *great* because of the extraordinary intensity and perfection of his poems."

Eastern European poetry, surrealist poetry, and other poetries in translation influenced Meyers. His Jewish heritage was also central to his identity as a writer. Born in 1928 in Los Angeles, Meyers dropped out of high school with the aim of becoming a poet. He read voraciously, wrote, befriended fellow writers, and worked as a house painter, a printer's apprentice, and as a picture framer and gilder. In 1964, he moved to Claremont, California, with his wife, son, and daughter. Meyers' wife, Odette, was the daughter of Polish Jews living in France. As a girl, she had been sent into the French countryside to live during World War II, where she posed as a Catholic to avoid falling into Nazi hands.

Although Meyers hadn't gone to college, he was admitted to graduate school at Claremont College on the merit of his poetry. Largely with the help of the publication of his second book of poems, *The Dark Birds* (Doubleday), Meyers began teaching at Pitzer College. I was lucky enough to take two poetry workshops from him at Pitzer. There is insufficient space here for me to properly acknowledge the impact being his student had on my life, but it was one of the most fortunate and important things that has ever happened to me.

The novelist and poet Dennis Cooper, who was also a student of Meyers, recounts a story that illustrates Meyers' irrepressible spirit and passionate devotion to poetry. "One day in early 1976," Cooper remembers, "I was wandering about the Pitzer campus with my nose in an ever-present—at that time—volume of Rimbaud's *A Season in Hell.* Bert and I crossed paths and began talking. Suddenly, in a gesture I can't forget, he grabbed me very firmly by the arm and told me that I was a hypocrite to read and worship Rimbaud while remaining within the kind of structure that Rimbaud despised and worked to overthrow. He told me to quit school, go to Paris, to either devote my life to poetry or to get out. I was startled by this reprimand but ultimately [was] convinced to do just what he said." Meyers' advice wouldn't have suited everyone, nor did I ever hear of him exhorting other students in a similar manner. For Cooper, it was just the shove he needed toward taking himself and his talent seriously.

Meyers' poem "The Drive" is a model of poetic control and restraint, fatalism, sharp observation, clarity, and lyric sadness. To my mind, there is nothing in the piece that is not perfectly suited to the poem, nothing that does not seamlessly further the little world it creates, its themes and effects. I defy any reader to find a superfluous note in it, yet the poem does not feel "tight," but rather graceful and easy to read. For me as a reader, it creates a quiet roar in the mind. Like much great writing, it is full of contradictions or apparent opposites: large/small, animal/human, open/closed, the calm/the erotic, indoors/outdoors, etc. Many of the words and images have double or triple meanings, beginning with the title, which, among other interpretations, could be taken to mean the drive the couple take in their car, sex drive, and humans' drive to dominate nature, or, as they are rather strangely instructed by God in Genesis, their need to "have dominion over . . . every living thing that

moveth upon the earth." There is such a ringing dignity, but no stuffi-
ness in the poem. The rhymes are not regularly occurring or showy, so
that one has to read it a few times to see that *shale* and *quail* link up,
and leap a stanza break to do it, and that *groaned* and *ground* echo each
other, as do *closed* and *clothes*. The ants bubbling out of the ground con-
stitute at once an image of a primordial volcano, a sexual event, and one
of the several images in the poem of an audience that is witnesse to the
sexual strivings of the humans in the poem.

I'd like to close with a quote from Meyers himself. "Some people
complained that my poems were too 'finished,' too tight from begin-
ning to end; that I left no room for the reader to use his imagination
. . . But, they misunderstood—they think mystery lies in the unfin-
ished and incomprehensible. To me, mystery lies in what seems to be
clear and finished. Such a poem implies an anxiety that seeks perfection
in order to avoid madness. One relieves anxiety by creating order and
perfection—but, since we know order and perfection don't really exist,
anxiety remains like a monster beneath the clear surface of artistic clas-
sicism—just listen to Mozart."

Cage

JOSEPHINE MILES

Through the branches of the Japanese cherry
Blooming like a cloud which will rain
A rain white as the sun
The living room across the roadway
Cuts its square of light
And in it fight
Two figures, hot, irate,
Stuck between sink and sofa in that golden cage.

Come out into the night, walk in the night,
It is for you, not me.
The cherry flowers will rain their rain as white
Cool as the moon.
Listen how they surround.
You swing among them in your cage of light.
Come out into the night.

DON BOGEN ON JOSEPHINE MILES' Cage

What struck me about "Cage" when I first saw it among the pre-
viously uncollected work in Josephine Miles's *Collected Poems 1930–83*
was its lyricism. Although Miles wrote lyric poetry all her life, she is
generally recognized as a poet more engaged with speech and ideas than
with song. Her interest in the American vernacular, from people yelling
at each other in traffic to bureaucratic jargon, informs her most well-
known pieces. These include thoughtful observations on academic life in
Berkeley, where she was a professor from the 1940s through the 1970s (no
poet is better on teaching and learning); explorations of philosophical
paradoxes; quirky takes on neighborhood life; and clear-eyed portraits of
a childhood marked by the arthritis that would leave her disabled—all
with her distinctive qualities of concision, wry humor, and an ear for the
way people talk. But "Cage" evinces a strand in her work that has largely
been overlooked, something more song-like and emotional.

What makes a good lyric? The tradition, of course, is immense, and
the poem must show awareness of it but not seem burdened by it. It
must be pared down, without the scaffolding of narrative, description
or character development that can support other poems. A good lyric
covers its tracks. Its movement must appear natural, even effortless. It
must convince through feeling more than argument. And, of course, it
must sing.

Miles meets these challenges with subtlety and grace. The surface of
"Cage" is simple—a tree, a street, a room—its progression from tension
to openness seemingly inevitable. The poem is built on contrasts—in-
side/outside, caged/open, light/dark, hot/cool—but these alone don't
account for its emotional effects. What makes the fight in the first stan-

za so disturbing, and what gives that sense of relief with the invitation to come outside in the second? Sentence use, for one thing. The fight scene is one long sentence suspended over eight lines, the invitation five short ones over seven. As the opening sentence builds, its focus shifts from the intricate beauty of the Japanese cherry inward to an increasingly limited scene: one square of light, two figures in it, bordered by two heavy fixtures. Closing the sentence on the title word "cage" seals the stanza in compacted tension, as if the poem were coiled around itself, unable to move. When the poet speaks to the couple in the second stanza, in contrast, her sentences are no longer constricted but balanced and open, with room for parallel constructions: "come out" and "walk," "you" and "me." Two two-line sentences are followed by three one-liners, ending the poem with a repetition not of the dilemma but of the invitation to escape it: "Come out into the night." Although the second stanza is one line shorter than the first, its five sentences make it feel longer and looser, as if the night offered endless possibilities.

One part of this invitation—a lure, if you will—is sensory. When the falling cherry petals come back in the second stanza, they no longer function just as visual images but take on the coolness of moonlight and a hushed, "surrounding" sound that encompasses both mystery and security. And then there's music. Miles flirts here with traditional patterns of rhyme and meter to find her own tune. The six full rhymes on "light," for example, set up a framework that serves to highlight the more subtle slant rhymes: "cherry/me," "rain/sun," and my favorite, "moon/surround." There is pleasure in recurrence and room for surprise, too. On a more dramatic level, the contrast between the harsh concluding *t*'s that reach their crescendo in the fight scene—"Cuts," "its," "light," "it," "fight," "hot," and "irate" in three short lines—and the more open *ooh* and *ow* sounds in the dreamiest part of the invitation—"you," "flowers," "cool," "moon," "how," "surround"—heightens the couple's tension and the promise of relief. Miles's music draws us into the evening.

It could be argued that all poems are finally about their makers, yet "Cage," for all its craft, does not focus on the poet's sensitivity. The direction it points is outward: "It is for you, not me." "Cage" shows a lyric side not commonly associated with Josephine Miles, but the generosity of spirit behind it is at the heart of her enterprise.

John Chapman

MARY OLIVER

He wore a tin pot for a hat, in which
he cooked his supper
toward evening
in the Ohio forests. He wore
a sackcloth shirt and walked
barefoot on feet crooked as roots. And everywhere he went
the apple trees sprang up behind him lovely
as young girls.

No Indian or settler or wild beast
ever harmed him, and he for his part honored
everything, all God's creatures thought little,
on a rainy night,
of sharing the shelter of a hollow log touching
flesh with any creatures there: snakes,
raccoon possibly, or some great slab of bear.

Mrs. Price, late of Richland County,
at whose parents' house he sometimes lingered,
recalled: he spoke
only once of women and his gray eyes
brittled into ice. "Some
are deceivers," he whispered, and she felt
the pain of it, remembered it
into her old age.

Well, the trees he planted or gave away
prospered, and he became
the good legend, you do
what you can if you can; whatever

the secret, and the pain,

there's a decision: to die,
or to live, to go on
caring about something. In spring, in Ohio,
in the forests that are left you can still find
sign of him: patches
of cold white fire.

R. T. SMITH ON MARY OLIVER'S John Chapman

On one brisk blue April day, after much-needed rain, I strolled out
to check our solitary winesap for blossoms and thought again of Mary
Oliver's poem "John Chapman," which remembers without quite re-
telling the story of that pioneer we often call Johnny Appleseed. After a
winter dormancy, our tree's young trunk and limbs were greening, and
a hundred buds showed their first hint of crimson. The sap inside was
shooting, and it was impossible not to imagine the satisfaction Chap-
man would have felt as thousands of trees he sold, gave away, or tended
himself began to open like sheer serendipity across a landscape once
sadly apple-poor.

It's not only the beauty of beginning that Oliver's poem celebrates
and savors. Inside her revisionist narrative, which skips across the man's
life like a stone across still water, a bitter seed attests to the complex-
ity of even a saintly existence. Of course, the association of apples with
discord comes as no surprise. In the biblical story, the serpent used the
apple of understanding to seduce Eve to disobedience, and she used the
same fruit to entice Adam to partake in her sin. From this simple act
much sorrow follows, as well as much relief—o felix culpa. We also cling
to other old and resonant stories featuring significant apples—Atalanta's
ruse, the judgment of Paris, Snow White's soporific—but it's the Eden
story Oliver employs to suggest the concealed cost of the abundant
beauty John Chapman broadcast.

Terse, simple words contribute to the opening tone, which is fairly in-
nocent, seemingly matter-of-fact and casual in a highly irregular free verse
that depends upon the poet's instinct for lyric patterns and the suspense
characteristic of narrative. The subject himself is modest, homespun, a
little goofy with his kettle helmet, but a sign of complication enters with

"sackcloth," which we associate with mourning. The pomologist's feet are bare and "crooked as roots," as if he were some penitent wandering the wilderness, and Oliver follows this suggestion of dissonance with the comparison between apple trees and young girls. Not especially surprising, as one thinks of pastel spring dresses and the whole history of the girls/blossoms metaphor, but these tree-girls springing up behind him seem potentially ominous, less innocent than simple dryads.

With the reader alert to the possibility of friction, Oliver shifts the poem back to the legend: because he is gentle and generous, Chapman is blessed. The aboriginal owners of the land he seeks to cultivate and the animals that roam those woods (emphatically labeled "all God's creatures!") allow him to pass unmolested. Holding to her severe Anglo-Saxon language, Oliver implies the mythic dimension by suggesting that even snakes and bears will tolerate his company, for he is a very different kind of hero than fabled contemporaries like Davy Crockett, who came to conquer.

The third stanza, which provides the center of the poem, delivers its unsettling insinuation of an explanation. Chapman, for some unspecified reason, has an axe to grind, and he does it cruelly on Mrs. Price. The scene is emotional, elliptical, as stark in silhouette as many of the scenes in Robert Penn Warren's similarly enigmatic historical poem "Audubon: A Vision." It's difficult not to connect the woman's name (Price) to her address (Richland) and suppose that Chapman's ethos runs somehow aslant of hers, but despite the commercial associations, she seems an innocent victim of his out-of-the-blue acidity. He does not indicate acceptance of present company when he delivers his judgment on women—"Some are deceivers." Those "eyes / brittled into ice," that calculated whisper, the unmistakable pain—she never forgets it. Never. If she had been a lovely girl springing up behind him, she would have withered at bloom and root, but she seems to know no more about his past encounters with women than the reader does.

The "well" with which the next stanza begins signals an awkwardness, a shift reminiscent of those we impose when conversation reaches a darkening impasse, but the narrator cannot banish the shadow. The admirable legend is tainted, humanized, damaged. One of the serious questions the poem begins to raise is whether this tincture of sorrow undermines or deepens the simple and valuable frontier wisdom: "you do what you can if you can." I believe the poem's "lesson" (though that word is too unriddled and bland to apply unmodified) becomes richer, more intricate, like a carefully grafted hybrid, due to this complication. Chapman's goodness, she suggests, his selfless energy, derives not from his life on the margins of civilization but from his frustrating engagement with society, emphasized by that one-line, insistent stanza, "the secret, and the pain."

The poem comes full circle. She has twice given us "pain" at the vexed and enigmatic center, but now Oliver returns us to "Ohio," "spring," and "forests," underscored this time with a difference. A new and crucial word eases in, addressing the reader. Who can witness, in the "remaining" (a note of regret for the vanished) forests, the startling flowering of apple trees? "You," the poet says. The reader is implicated, and what he or she sees beatifying the woodlands is an enigma, a fire that is "cold" and "white." Pain and pleasure, beauty and harm, the bad with the good. "Nothing gold can stay." So many associations soar in on the wings of that little complication between the words "cold" and "fire."

In a less stark, more domesticated poem, the central paradox might register as ironic: the provident sower, the agent of nourishing increase, operated from a wounded psyche. The philanthropist harbors the bitter seed of misogyny, so the brightness that remains his legacy seems cold, the fruitfulness dependent upon retreat, even an element of sterility. But here, irony is too cerebral a response, for the twist in Chapman's heart is a reminder of something elemental, however well camouflaged. Injured people often make beauty by the method and motives that drive an oyster to create a pearl. Perhaps John Chapman fell into that category.

This psychological snarl in the weave subverts the anticipated pastoral of a poem about Johnny Appleseed and sustains the poem in my mind. Although "John Chapman" first appeared in the prominent *American Scholar* and helps establish the bridge between the historical and the natural in Oliver's Pulitzer Prize volume, *American Primitive* (Atlantic-Little Brown, 1983), it does not appear in her *New and Selected Poems,* and I have never seen this poem in an anthology. It is not an easy poem to forget, and I hope that readers continue to find its white fire. In an April week, when harvest is only a distant whisper and I see the one young tree in my yard and imagine the hundreds across the county, the thousands blossoming across the swath Chapman traveled, it is not Frost's weariness with the ladders and the cider heaps that fill my dreams but Oliver's provident but blemished eremite, the sure-footed reticence of her poem with its ambitiously modest exhortation: "you do what you can if you can."

Psalm

GEORGE OPPEN

Veritas sequitur . . .

In the small beauty of the forest
The wild deer bedding down—
That they are there!

Their eyes
Effortless, the soft lips
Nuzzle and the alien small teeth
Tear at the grass

The roots of it
Dangle from their mouths
Scattering earth in the strange woods.
They who are there.

Their paths
Nibbled thru the fields, the leaves that shade them
Hang in the distances
Of sun

     The small nouns
Crying faith
In this in which the wild deer
Startle, and stare out.

A psalm? How so? When I first discovered it, I held George Oppen's "Psalm" suspect as one of those poems about very little at all—one whose title, implying substance, in fact hopes to "cover" the poem's absence of it. The modes of psalm being two—praise and lament—I was willing to take the poem, at best, as simply an act of witnessing some deer, witness as a form of recognition, recognition as a form of deeming a thing worth recognizing: perhaps a stretch, but a kind of praise, anyway, for one of God's creatures—given the cues of the title and epigraph, that we should read this poem through the lens of theology. As for lament—well, I found none.

But the epigraph's reference to Aquinas notwithstanding, it was via Gerard Manley Hopkins that I came to read the poem differently and to appreciate more fully the relationship between syntax and narrative. Hopkins discusses (in "The Principle or Foundation") the praising of God, and the different options for praise available to humans as opposed to the rest of creation. A key difference is that the latter

> glorify God, *but they do not know it.* The birds sing to him, the thunder speaks of his terror . . . the honey [is] like his sweetness . . . they give him glory, but they do not know they do . . . they never can . . . But man can know God, *can mean to give him glory.* This then was why he was made, to give God glory and to mean to give it . . . (italics his)

By this reasoning, then, it is enough for the deer, "That they are there!": their praise is manifest in their deer-ness itself, be it in the form of tearing at the grass or "merely" startling, and staring out. But in the shift in phrasing that occurs from "That they are there!" to "They who are there."—from the ecstasy of exclamation, whose punctuation makes the fragment seem somehow complete and/or expected, to the stranded relative clause whose punctuation, in suggesting the end of a finished sentence, throws the fragmentedness into greater relief—in this shift, a stall seems at work, at the level of syntax: a moment of reassessing more soberly what had earlier been surprised outburst. I believe that this is where Oppen faces squarely the notion that humans have a greater responsibility, when it comes to praise. Humans have the ability to *articulate* praise, via language, and therefore a duty to do so.

Syntax is the chief tool that language has for conveying meaning. And it is at the level of syntax that Oppen puts forward his concerns about praise, our obligation to give praise, and the limits to our ability to do so. Throughout the poem, there are what I'll call dislocations in the syntax, places where this syntax—as if inevitably—gets derailed. Technically, for example, the subordinate clause "Their eyes / Effortless" must modify "the soft lips," but that makes no sense. "They who are there" takes us back to the deer only because the phrase so closely resembles line three, which described the deer; but by conventional syntax, the phrase must refer back to the "strange woods" of line ten. Again, sense is strained. Another dangling modifier occurs at stanza four, whose "Their paths / Nibbled thru the fields" seems to modify "the leaves that shade them." When we get to "the small nouns" of the final stanza, they seem to refer to the deer again, until we realize that the deer won't appear for another couple of lines; are the small nouns, then, the "distances / Of sun," or the leaves, or the fields, or the paths through them?

The syntax both embodies and enacts a constant feinting, a casting outward—only to fall short, each time, of "complete" meaning. The tension between the attempt to mean and the routine failure to *entirely* mean becomes emblematic of a parallel tension: between the duty we have to try to praise God to the best of our capacities and the limitations to those capacities, finally, insofar as we are human—small nouns—and therefore necessarily flawed.

In its immediate content, Oppen's poem is an act of praise in the form of granting witness. At the level of syntax, the poem articulates the gesture itself of praise, of attempting to give it; and it articulates the inadequacy inherent to that attempt and subtly laments that inadequacy. Praise and lament. And a persuasive example of how syntax can generate and sustain the psychological narrative of a poem. And Oppen's "Psalm"? A psalm, indeed.

The Hardness Scale

JOYCE PESEROFF

Diamonds are forever so I gave you quartz
which is #7 on the hardness scale
and it's hard enough to get to know anybody these days
if only to scratch the surface
and quartz will scratch six other mineral surfaces:
it will scratch glass
it will scratch gold
it will even
scratch your eyes out one morning—you can't be
too careful.
Diamonds are industrial so I bought
a ring of topaz
which is #8 on the hardness scale.
I wear it on my right hand, the way it was
supposed to be, right? No tears and fewer regrets
for reasons smooth and clear as glass. Topaz will scratch glass,
it will scratch your quartz,
and all your radio crystals. You'll have to be silent
the rest of your days
not to mention your nights. Not to mention
the night you ran away very drunk very
very drunk and you tried to cross the border
but couldn't make it across the lake.
Stirring up geysers with the oars you drove the red canoe
in circles, tried to pole it but
your left hand didn't know
what the right hand was doing.
You fell asleep
and let everyone know it when you woke up.
In a gin-soaked morning (hair of the dog) you went
hunting for geese,
shot three lake trout in violation of the game laws,
told me to clean them and that
my eyes were bright as sapphires

which is #9 on the hardness scale.
A sapphire will cut a pearl
it will cut stainless steel
it will cut vinyl and mylar and will probably
cut a record this fall
to be released on an obscure label known only to aficionados.
I will buy a copy.
I may buy you a copy
depending on how your tastes have changed.
I will buy copies for my friends
we'll get a new needle,
a diamond needle,
which is #10 on the hardness scale
and will cut anything.
It will cut wood and mortar,
plaster and iron,
it will cut the sapphires in my eyes and I will bleed
blind as 4 A.M. in the subways when even degenerates
are dreaming, blind as the time
you shot up the room with a new hunting rifle
blind drunk
as you were.
You were #11 on the hardness scale
later that night
apologetic as
you worked your way up
slowly from the knees
and you worked your way down
from the open-throated blouse.
Diamonds are forever so I give you softer things.

LLOYD SCHWARTZ ON JOYCE PESEROFF'S The Hardness Scale

In her poem "The Hardness Scale," Joyce Peseroff pulls the rug over our eyes while she's pulling the wool out from under us. This unsentimental twentieth-century love poem (among its reference points

are a crystal set and a turntable with a diamond needle) has its liter-
ary roots in both seventeenth-century metaphysical poetry and Borscht
Belt one-liners. It's hard to believe such a beautifully crafted, delicious-
ly funny, and surprisingly touching cornucopia of contradictions isn't
in every poetry anthology. First printed in the landmark 1975 issue of
Ploughshares Frank Bidart guest-edited, it then became the title poem of
Peseroff's first book (Alice James, 1977), which has recently been reis-
sued by Carnegie Mellon.

The poem is triggered by a commercial—De Beers' still-inescap-
able slogan pitching diamonds as the epitome of romance, the ideal
expression of love ("A kiss on the hand," Lorelei Lee sings in *Gentlemen
Prefer Blondes,* "may be quite continental, but diamonds are a girl's best
friend"). Peseroff begins with the ad's seductive promise, "Diamonds
are forever." But by mid-line, the gentle flow of smoothly falling ca-
dences starts to stutter; the rhythm reverses itself into cheeky monosyl-
lables, ironically undercutting the possibility of romance with the slap
of reality, the schpritz in the kisser: "So I gave you quartz."

That advertising phrase also sets up Peseroff's basic image: Moh's
scale of mineral density, from 1 to 10, on which talc is the softest at #1
and diamonds are the hardest at #10. It's as resonant and productive an
image as John Donne's pair of "stiff twin compasses" in his "Valediction
Forbidding Mourning," another love poem that uses unexpected scien-
tific imagery to measure an emotional relationship.

One of the joys of "The Hardness Scale" is its slipperiness. It just
won't stay put. Peseroff keeps reminding us, elbowing us, that this is
Writing we're reading. Just like Keats at the end of "Ode to a Night-
ingale," when he writes a word ("forlorn"), then immediately responds
to it, comments on it ("Forlorn! The very word is like a bell . . ."), ac-
knowledges the fact that he's writing a poem by referring to the word
he's just come up with; so, when Peseroff says that quartz is "#7 on the
hardness scale," mentioning hardness reminds her that

> it's hard enough to get to know anybody these days
> if only to scratch the surface . . .

One good cliché deserves another; which forces us to take them all more
literally; which energizes the tired language, brings the inventiveness of
the original image back to life; which brings us back, refreshed, to the

central image: "and quartz will scratch six other mineral surfaces." And if anyone thought that low-stakes science jokes were all we were going to be dealt, our eyes are soon forced violently open to that misapprehension:

> it will scratch glass
> it will scratch gold
> it will even
> scratch your eyes out one morning—you can't be
> too careful.

Gradually, we get to know the happy/unhappy couple in this complicated, complicitly co-dependent sexual relationship. Do they thrive on scratching each other's surfaces? They have an agreement about "commitment," a modern understanding:

> Diamonds are industrial so I bought
> a ring of topaz
> which is #8 on the hardness scale.
> I wear it on my right hand, the way it was
> supposed to be, right? No tears and fewer regrets . . .

The best joke comes near the end. Guess what's #11 on the hardness scale, harder even than diamonds? And at the very end, even this joke gets undercut with the most mysteriously moving and profound moment in the poem—the plangent, unforgettable last line, which offers once and for all and unequivocally the essential secret of love.

Mad Girl's Love Song

SYLVIA PLATH

I shut my eyes and all the world drops dead;
I lift my lids and all is born again.
(I think I made you up inside my head.)

The stars go waltzing out in blue and red,
And arbitrary blackness gallops in:
I shut my eyes and all the world drops dead.

I dreamed that you bewitched me into bed
And sung me moon-struck, kissed me quite insane.
(I think I made you up inside my head.)

God topples from the sky, hell's fires fade:
Exit Seraphim and Satan's men:
I shut my eyes and all the world drops dead.

I fancied you'd return the way you said.
But I grow old and I forget your name.
(I think I made you up inside my head.)

I should have loved a thunderbird instead;
At least when spring comes they roar back again.
I shut my eyes and all the world drops dead.
(I think I made you up inside my head.)

MARY JO BANG ON SYLVIA PLATH'S Mad Girl's Love Song

    In May, 1953, Sylvia Plath's college journal, *The Smith Review,* published three of her villanelles; one was "Mad Girl's Love Song." To celebrate that occasion (along with other recent successes), Olive Prouty, Plath's benefactress, invited Plath, her mother, and her brother, Warren, to tea. The poem would reappear in the August issue of *Mademoiselle,* at whose offices Plath had served in June—along with twenty other selected coeds—a month-long guest editorship. That editorship would famously antedate her clinical depression and suicide attempt by two months and would ultimately provide the seeds for her autobiographic novel, *The Bell Jar*. In August, after leaving a note saying she'd gone for a long walk and would be "home tomorrow," she took a glass of water and a bottle of sleeping pills to the basement where she secreted herself in a crawl space with a blanket and lost consciousness. After the fact of her being found days later, dehydrated but alive, the managing editor of *Mademoiselle*, Cyrilly Abels, called Mrs. Plath to express her concern and apologize for having given a Boston tabloid a copy of "Mad Girl's Love Poem" to print alongside the notice of Sylvia's suicide attempt.

All of which gives the poem's appearance in print, thrice in quick succession, a powerful biographical anchor. One finds a later mention of the poem amid Plath's voluminous journal entries—on March 10, 1956, two weeks after the well-documented meeting between Plath and her future husband, Ted Hughes, at a Cambridge (England) party. In a postscript to a previous entry the same day, Plath invokes the poem as a way of describing her current state of fevered and thankless waiting for Hughes to show himself: "Postscript: Oh the fury, the fury. Why did I even know he was here. The panther wakes and stalks again, and every sound in the house is his tread on the stair; I wrote "Mad Girl's Love Song" once in a mad mood like this when Mike didn't come and didn't come, and every time I am dressed in black, white, and red: violent, fierce colors. All the steps coming up and running past I made into his step and cursed the usurpers that took his place . . ." In 1957, the poem appeared in the British journal *Granta*. Then, but for its inclusion in the occasional anthology of villanelles, its history in print ends. While Plath is said to have stood behind the poem to those who would later be asked, she chose not to include it in her 1960 *The Colossus and Other Poems*, and Hughes left it out of the posthumously published *Ariel*—as well as out of the later *Crossing the Water* and the later still *Winter*. He fails to list it among the pre-1956 works in the Juvenilia section of *The Collected* without mistakenly adding it to the post-. There is no way to know why.

Given its adolescent beginnings, it might be tempting to read the poem as a minor mirror of adolescent turmoil (as the Boston tabloid's pairing suggests), but to do so seems to me a mistake. It is perfectly virtuosic in its technical brilliance yet never seems a mere exercise. There are those who speculate it was at least partly the result of a verse forms class Plath was taking at Smith at the time. Regardless, the poem is a pie: a perfect marriage between form and filling. Villanelles, a French verse form of an Italian folk song, are said to have a peasant dance rhythm. With their persistently interwoven refrains and nearly totally unrelenting rhyme, they also have the obsessive rhythm of the well-known, near-psychotic state of infatuation—a state of mind and being usually first experienced in adolescence, but rarely limited to it.

"I shut my eyes and all the world drops dead." The lines are accentually and syllabically perfect—five beats, ten syllables, with the slyest fall away from meter at the point when, in the second line of the fourth stanza, Satan and Seraphim both exit. It seems formally right that the line should register the seismic shift. And it does: the initial weak syllable of the iamb is absent—causing the "Ex" of "Exit" to stand alone on a truncated monosyllabic foot. The syllable count is reduced by one, just as the mad girl's world would be if the beloved only existed "in her head." The truncated syllable also echoes the annihilation the mad girl effects in the first line by simply closing her eyes. Freud's Id is poised for survival. What can't be controlled, made to come on time and when needed so passionately, can simply be blinked out. That is both the wish and the fear. Biographic outcomes aside, it's the seed of psychological truth buried in the staccato of a state of continual rumination that raises the poem above mere virtuosity or girlish practice for a later, better poem.

The Craftsmen of the Little Box

VASKO POPA

TRANSLATED BY CHARLES SIMIC

Don't open the little box
Heaven's hat will fall out of her

Don't close her for any reason
She'll bite the trouser leg of eternity

Don't drop her on the earth
The sun's eggs will break inside her

Don't throw her in the air
Earth's bones will break inside her

Don't hold her in your hands
The dough of the stars will go sour inside her

What are you doing for God's sake
Don't let her get out of your sight

ALAN MICHAEL PARKER ON VASKO POPA'S Little Box Series

What to do with the Surrealist poem? I love its anomie, claustro-phobia, and whimsy; I'm seduced by the prospects of the aesthetics, how such a poem tenders both innovation and intrigue. The Surrealist poem is a sexy poem, with its presentation of apparently dissociated in-formation supercharged by the unconscious.

But the Surrealist poem also seems—at least to me, as a poem I might write—a kind of cop-out. Neither automatic writing nor the joys of chance allow me enough choice, and thus the results seem less intel-lectually present than I believe my poems need to be. Where's the formal invention? Where are the ideas? Is it possible for my work to be about ideas and offer innovation, intrigue, and the wildness of the Surrealists?

As a neophyte in 1979, I first read Charles Simic and Mark Strand's groundbreaking 1976 anthology of poets and fabulists from Europe and South America, *Another Republic*. This book at once became a primer for me, not only because I was privileged to hear William Gass lecture on some of these writers but also because their work immediately mattered in ways I have spent more than twenty years trying to understand. Among these writers—many of whom I continue to love, including Zbigniew Herbert, Octavio Paz, Yehuda Amichai, Nicanor Parra, and Italo Calvino—I discovered the poems of the Yugoslav poet Vasko Popa, considered (at least in the West) to be the most important Serbian poet of the twentieth century. But such an unofficial title guarantees little: Popa remains widely unread among American poetry readers.

Born in 1922 in the village of Vojvodina, Popa was well educated, graduating from the University in Belgrade's Faculty of Philosophy in 1949. A concentration camp survivor with a grim wit, Popa was deeply committed to Serbian history, folklore, and mythology. Until his death in 1991, Popa was a prominent literary figure and editor; his major work as a poet occurred in various series and featured recurring characters, including, most notably, a lame wolf, St. Sava, and my favorite, the little box.

Popa's spare "Little Box" series offers a cosmology, a world constrained and liminal, fraught with fundamental questions of being. Violence recurs: The little box seems constantly at risk, beset by political forces and what may well be government or police action. Ultimately, then, these nifty Cold War parables resonate within their historical moment as well as existentially.

But a wildness persists, too, amidst Popa's pared-down music and his complex use of repetition (formal elements that seem simple and yet innovative). "Don't open the little box / Heaven's hat will fall out of her" begins "The Craftsmen of the Little Box." Such a surprising leap, the little box becoming a hat box for heaven, resonates more powerfully because it moves us logically beyond our own expectations—and there lies Popa's debt to Surrealism. While not a Surrealist, Popa mines the Surrealist aesthetic for a certain wildness—a wildness that serves as counterpoint to his rigorous intellectual and political musings.

"Blandula, Tenella, Vagula"

EZRA POUND

What has thou, O my soul, with paradise?
Will we not rather, when our freedom's won,
Get us to some clear place wherein the sun
Lets drift in on us through the olive leaves
A liquid glory? If at Sirmio,
My soul, I meet thee, when this life's outrun,
Will we not find some headland consecrated
By aery apostles of terrene delight,
Will not our cult be founded on the waves,
Clear sapphire, cobalt, cyanine,
On triune azures, the impalpable
Mirrors unstill of the eternal change?

Soul, if She meet us there, will any rumour
Of havens more high and courts desirable
Lure us beyond the cloudy peak of Riva?[1]

SUSAN WHEELER ON EZRA POUND'S "Blandula, Tenella, Vagula"

At eighteen, when I first read this poem, I had only just decided
that the best state in which to be writing poems was akin to that of do-
ing long-division problems. Poetry—in its best sense—was like math,
I thought: clear, unclouded, absorbing, and cooly *blue*. The writing of
it transported the writer to a limpid place of crystalline thought, where
the air was rarefied and the words were "aery apostles of terrene de-
light." This poem's "triune azures" and "mirrors unstill" created such a
place for me, and the poem's final question embodied both a doubt and
a yearning I found very moving.

That the poem's title, with its nonce *tenella,* alluded the Emperor
Hadrian's dying address to his soul, "Animula vagula blandula" (or "O
blithe little soul, flitting away"), meant little to me; I knew nothing of
Sirmio or Riva, places on a lake in Italy where the Latin poet Catullus
had stayed; and Catullus himself, I knew from beans at the time. These

references muddied the water even while establishing, with their proper nouns, a kind of veracity.

Ezra Pound loved Catullus. "The most hard-edged and intense of the Latin poets,"[2] Pound wrote about the man who had written lines such as

> I'll fuck the pair of you as you prefer it,
> oral Aurelius, anal Furius,
> who read my verses but misread their author:
> you think that *I'm* effeminate, since *they* are.[3]

but also lyrics like his own paean to his father's villa on Sirmio, a promontory on the southern shore of Lago dí Garda, a place from which he could look out across the intensely blue water to see the peaks of the lower Alps on the northern shore, just beyond the town of Riva. Far from being a still idyll, Sirmio (now called Sirmione) is windy and changeable, with dramatic light and cloud formations, mutable weather. In 56 B.C., Catullus had returned to it after a rough year of civil service in Bithynia. Home at last, he could write:

> The mind puts down her load and, tired with travel,
> We come to our Lares and rest in our own beds.
> This is really all we undertake these toils for![4]

So, in the spring of 1909, in his early twenties, Ezra Pound—who had long left behind Philadelphia for London and courted favor with Yeats—came to Sirmione, checked in at Hotel Eden (over the years, he returned frequently to this hotel, bringing other guests, including James Joyce), and grafted his ambition to that of Catullus. He could "lie on what is left of Catullus' parlour floor and speculate the azure beneath it and the hills off to Salo and Riva with their forgotten gods moving unhindered amongst them . . ."[5]

As I've gotten older, I have come to appreciate how profound (and, sometimes, how *unintended*) a poet's affinity with older poets can be, and this element of the poem alone moves me greatly now. In spite of Pound's transgressions—broadcasting for Italy's fascists during the war, a roiling anti-Semitism—I have never been able to shake his own influence on me. Pound also wrote about Sirmio not only in allegiance to Catullus but also in disavowal of the Victorians: his was an antidote to the several wordier poems about Sirmio by Tennyson and Gosse, Binyon, Hardy, and Swinburne. The poem incorporates Pound's vision of a new poetry, a new language, fresh and vigorous despite its massive inheritance.

However, it is the paradise in the poem that prevails. This is the earthly paradise the gods watch over, earthly as it is even in the afterlife of the soul, and the clear sapphire, cobalt, cyanine are but the reflective elements which will fuse, in our vision, our selves with all that is clear and constituted by thought. It is in having made manifest *this* yearning—for our souls to be inseparable from our faith, for their fusion with God in whatever way we conceive of the "triune azures"—that the poem continues to bowl me over.

1. Ezra Pound, *Personae: The Collected Shorter Poems of Ezra Pound,* New Directions, 1971, p. 39.

2. Ezra Pound, Letter to Harriet Monroe, Feb. 1916, *Selected Letters 1907–1941,* New Directions, 1971, p. 69.

3. Catullus, #XVI, translated by Charles Martin, *The Poems of Catullus,* The Johns Hopkins University Press, 1990, p. 19.

4. Catullus, #XXXI, translated by C. H. Sisson, *The Poetry of Catullus,* The Orion Press, 1967, p. 49.

5. From *Poetry Review,* 1912, pp. 72–73, as quoted in *A Guide to Ezra Pound's Personae (1926)* by K. K. Ruthven, University of California Press, 1969, p. 47.

The Moonflower

F. T. PRINCE

The secret drops of love run though my mind:
Midnight is filled with sounds of the full sea
That has risen softly among the rocks:
Air stirs the cedar-tree.

Somewhere a fainting sweetness is distilled:
It is the moonflower hanging in its tent
Of twisted broad-leaved branches by the stony path
That squanders the cool scent.

Pallid, long as a lily, it swings a little
As if drunk with its own perfume and the night,
Which draws its perfume out and leaves the flower
The weaker for its flight.

Detached from my desires, in an oblivion
Of this world that surrounds me, in weariness
Of all but darkness, silence, starry solitude,
I too feel that caress—

Delicate, serene and peaceful, lonely, strange
To the intellect and the imagination,
The touch with which reality wounds and ravishes
Our inmost desolation.

All being like the moonflower is dissatisfied
For the dark kiss that the night only gives,
And night gives only to the soul that waits in longing
And in that only lives.

JOHN ASHBERY ON F. T. PRINCE'S The Moonflower

F. T. Prince is a poet who deserves to be better known. Born in South Africa in 1912, he studied there and at Oxford and matured in England in the 1930s. It was an exciting period for poetry: Auden, Mac-Neice, Spender, and others were producing their finest work. Prince was just a few years younger than they and participated in the scene, though always somewhat on the fringes. His first book, *Poems,* was published in 1938 by Faber and Faber.

He was distanced from his contemporaries by a number of factors, including temperament, leading a fairly isolated life in Southampton, England, where he taught at the University for many years. He died in 2004, survived by his wife, Elizabeth, and two daughters. Growing up far from the centers of poetry, he was free to form his own poetic allegiances. Unlike Auden, for instance, who lived in Germany and seems to have had little use for French poetry, Prince was drawn to the work of Rimbaud and Valery and to T. S. Eliot's translation of St.-John Perse's epic prose poem, *Anabase.* He also read extensively in Italian literature of the Renaissance, which resulted in a classic study of the Italian elements in Milton's verse (Milton being another poet who was out of favor in 1930s England).

"The Moonflower," the early poem I have chosen, is a flawless gem, like several scattered throughout English poetry: One thinks of the anonymous ballad "The Unquiet Grave," of Southwell's "The Burning Babe," of Keats's "grasshopper" sonnet, of Emily Dickinson's "Because I could not stop for death." Like those, it is both very simple and mysterious. The hushed, almost oppressive nocturnal sweetness suggests Keats's "Ode to a Nightingale." But Prince is more oblique. From the very first line—one of the greatest first lines in English poetry, I submit—one wonders: what are those secret drops? What exactly is this moonflower, that "squanders" its scent, and is left "the weaker" by the night that draws out its perfume? And what exactly is the role of the night? It provides the poet, both weary and ecstatic, with a haven, a medium for the caress of the moonflower: "Delicate, serene and peaceful, lonely, strange / To the intellect and the imagination"—an isolated place indeed!

The last stanza is the most mysterious and, paradoxically, the most rewarding. All being (along with the moonflower) is dissatisfied—dissatisfied for the dark kiss that only night gives. Strange, to be dissatisfied *for* something. And the final couplet compounds the mystery. Does night give only to the soul that waits in longing, and lives in that (i.e., the soul)? Or is it the soul that waits and lives only in longing? I suppose it's the latter, but the wording is such that it might indeed be night that needs to live in the longing soul. I think that it's probably a functional ambiguity: the soul and the night depend on each other, can only live within each other. In any case, the ecstasy seems not unlike that of St. John of the Cross (whose poetry Prince has translated): sacred and profane woven together in a single strand.

Epilogue

N. H. PRITCHARD

F O LL O WING THE   C ALM
HARKEN IN G CRYSTALS SP   READ
    T HEIR LIGHT
G ONE W AS S WEPT A WAY
THE   O T HER   S WAND ERE D ON

T HERE WE RE   T RACES OF SO UND
NO W   AND A GAIN
A GAIN
A GA IN
WOUND AB OUT THE rA IN
N EVER
CAME
A GAIN THE   LANES LAY
A GAIN

S   C A T T E R E D
A R E
T H E
G R A V E S
B RAVE C HILLS S IN K THE
    W I   L L
A GAIN
A GAIN
S TILL
A GAIN

L ON G SINCE H AS THE   STORM
    G ONE
ASI DUO S L L Y EARS UN FOLD
THEIR   R I N G S
BE NEAT H T HE   B ARK
EDGES   DARK   EN

```
SUCH   T  HA  T   IS   IS   SUCH
THAT   ON   E   W   IT   H   OUT   ON   E
SIMPLY   S   H   H   H   H   H   H   H   H   H   UN
THE   R   E   S   T
P   ESTER   IN   G   THE   L   EAVES
B   EST   TO   HAVE   R   E   S   T   E   D
B   E   L   I   E   V   I   N   G
IN   A   S   EE   D
```

Bryn Mawy
February
1967

CHARLES BERNSTEIN ON N. H. PRITCHARD'S Epilogue

Poets can be more or less overlooked: known but not well known, like Willy Loman on a pipefitter's holiday; known in their day but lost to us now; recovered or, if not, recovering. For every emerging poet a couple of others begin to fade; we even begin to fade to ourselves, if the truth be told. We know of the poet's poet and even hear from time to time of the poet's poet's poet, repeating, more in relief than disappointment, John Ashbery's famous quip that a famous poet is not famous. But poetry's "disappeared," as Ron Silliman once called them, haunt us, less from a fear for ourselves than a dread that the context that imparts meaning to our work is so fragile. *I* is not an *other* but many others, our fellow travelers among the dead, near-dead, and just about alive.

I found N. H. (Norman) Pritchard's *The Matrix: Poems 1960–1970* just a few years ago at the Ark, a used book store on the Upper West Side of Manhattan. It is an elegant clothbound book with a large photo of Pritchard, featuring his elegant handlebar moustache—he looks a bit like a soulful Salvador Dali—staring, eerily, from the front cover (or is it from the great beyond?). The book was published by Doubleday in 1970 but the only sustained references I know to Pritchard's work are A. L. Nielsen's immensely useful discussion in his 1997 *Black Chant: Languages of African-American Postmodernism* and a much earlier essay by Lorenzo Thomas, "The Shadow World: New York's Umbra Workshop & Origins of the Black Arts Movement," published in *Callaloo* in 1978. (Nielsen mentions a 1992 essay by Kevin Young, "Signs of Repression: N. H. Pritchard's *The Matrix*".)

The Matrix is a strikingly designed volume, composed of seventy-one poems in three parts, mostly visual or "concrete" poems, which are at the same time "sound" poems. It is one of the most interesting works of its kind from this period of American poetry. Nielsen mentions the connection to scat, a jazz vocalist's style of intoning "vocables" (vocal sounds not immediately processed as words), while Thomas notes the connection with the "vocal styles and tones" of African languages. Pritchard hops, skips, and jumps with his syncopated words, creating spaces inside words in a way that makes one word many. It's a rhythmic concatenation that relies on multiplicity and ambiguity. When I first read these poems I realized Pritchard was a perfect example of the "ideolectical," about which I write in "The Poetics of the Americas" in *My Way: Speeches and Poems.* The ideolectical is meant to suggest a synthesis of dialect and idiolect, centering on the use of nonstandard words and syntax—whether invented or based on the vernacular.

The opening page of *The Matrix* gives virtually all the information I know about Pritchard: Born in New York City in 1939, graduated from NYU, published in *Umbra* (a crucial magazine of the Black Arts movement), *The New Black Poetry,* and *The East Village Other.* He also performs his poetry on the 1967 Broadside album, compiled by Walter Lowenfels, *New Jazz Poets.* The bio ends with a notice that he teaches a workshop at the New School and is poet-in-residence at Friends Seminary.

Subsequently, I found a copy of his second book, *EECCHHOOEESS,* published by NYU Press in 1971. The book continues the complex, often letter-for-letter linguistic, visual, and sound play of *The Matrix.* Taken together, Pritchard's two books anticipate several of the formally inventive techniques that would gain greater circulation in the U.S. later in the '70s, though his work is almost never referenced in these contexts because, within a few years of these two books, the work seemed to disappear from the poetry horizon. (I recognize the circular reasoning here: lack of reference erases, the erased are not well enough known to reference; after all, the work was out there to find.)

Other traces of Pritchard: a magnificent, very short piece on a 1999 album by Bill Dixon, playing with Tony Oxley, entitled "Quadro Di

N. H. Pritchard"; I am listening to it now—and the majestic space between each note seems to open up a universe inside the one we so often think we are living in. The album is called *Papyrus* and it reminds me about what is not yet lost in our vast trove of paper and digital archives: if only we know were to look or how to read what we find.

Over time, in which we are all lost, some words, or almost words, jolt us, jam us, join us, as this from *EECCHHOOEESS:*

> junt
> mool oio clash brodge
> cense anis oio
> mek me isto plawe

[— — ——————]

MAN RAY

DEAN YOUNG ON MAN RAY'S [— — ——————]

Dada in all its manifestations was marked by a drive to sabotage that arose out of disgust and verges on tantrum. "Murder and madness were rampant," wrote Hans Arp. Looking everywhere and seeing nothing but nineteenth-century pieties mobilized to send thousands to a mechanized, pointless slaughter that benefited no one but a few fat cats, Dada was the first true realism of the twentieth century. The monstrosities of Hanna Hoch's collages mirrored the reconstructed faces and experimental prostheses clattering through the streets and propped up in cafes like the poisoned flotsam of a botched mass suicide. The cacophonous performances of simultaneously declaimed nonsense poems, piano pummelings, and pictures drawn and immediately erased or torn apart only differed from the snarl of political posturings, tactical idiocies, and social lies in that in Dada no one got killed: everyone was already limping anyway. "It's a fucked-up foolish world," diagnosed Richard Huelsenbeck. "Let's shit multi-colors," proposed Tristan Tzara. Against such a profound sense of the pointlessness and bankruptcy of life, there was only one thing to do: throw a party like a grenade, make an art of destruction, make a celebration of mockery. "Revolted by the butchery of the 1914 World War, we devoted ourselves to the arts: we were seeking art based on fundamentals, to cure the madness of the age," avowed Arp. Or at least trepan it.

Exhibit A: Man Ray's poem endures with a frontal assault that makes the avant-garde pretensions of today seem like wormy appeals for tenure. Has he succeeded in writing a poem that reaches that most unlikely of goals: to be understood by all? Certainly the poem is written in a universal language. You don't even have to know how to read to read it! Even the translations I have seen, from the French into Italian, into German and English preserve all its effects; nothing is lost. Its measure and musicality remain unalterable. The poem reaches a level of originality that defeats ownership and individuality. Like the readymades of Man Ray's henchman Marcel Duchamp, the poem slips all our forms of authentification, dumbfounding us in self-consuming confabulations of aesthetic judgment. All poetry depends upon an interchange between opacity and translucence. To some degree, all poetry must create impenetrability, otherwise the words are only indicators of things beyond them and, therefore, of diminished importance. Some poets create opacity through excess luminosity like Gerard Manley Hopkins, whose stylistic wattage sets up impediments to getting the poem's content. Man Ray's poem achieves opacity purely through an extremity of blackness, of ink which irrationally becomes utterly lucid. All poetry is a form of encryptment, and the reading of poetry is much like breaking a code. Here the code has achieved a sort of purity: it cannot be broken, yet the severity of its encryptment, its hiddenness, leads to clarity. The poem is blunt in presenting a series of signs that stand for everything that is deleted, defeated, and cannot be divulged. Maybe there is nothing left in the graves of civilization worth exhuming. Maybe there is no confession that can atone. The message has already been cut from the doughboy's letter home because, finally, all information is too sensitive or there is no message to send anymore. This is a poem at the end of all poetry, when everything is crossed out, the ultimate revision, the perfect imperfection, the antipode to Mallarme's perfect blank. Yet it could also not be the interpolated outcome of revisionist zeal, a disowning of the past, so much as a recapitulation, a total welcoming, the culmination of a culture that builds on itself, the last density that allows nothing to escape.

Shakespeare under Donne under Jonson under Herrick under Milton under Marvell under Swift under Blake under Keats under Tennyson under Browning under under under. Or maybe it's just a dark joke.

Nine Poems
for the unborn child
MURIEL RUKEYSER

I

The childless years alone without a home
Flashed daily with the world's glimpse, happiness.
Always behind was the dark screen of loss
Hardly moving, like heavy hardly-moving cloud.
"Give me myself," or "Take me," I said aloud;
There was little to give, and always less to take.
Except the promise, except the promise darkness
Makes, night and daylight, miracle to come.
Flying over, I suddenly saw the traces
Of man : where man is, you may read the wind
In shadow and smoke, know how the wind is gone
And know the way of man;   in the fall of the plane
Into its levels, encounter the ancient spaces:
The fall to life, the cliff and strait of bone.

II

They came to me and said, "There is a child."
Fountains of images broke through my land.
My swords, my fountains spouted past my eyes
And in my flesh at last I saw.   Returned
To when we drove in the high forest, and earth
Turned to glass in the sunset where the wild
Trees struck their roots as deep and visible
As their high branches, the double planted world.

"There is no father," they came and said to me.
—-I have known fatherless children, the searching, walk
The world, look at all faces for their father's life.
Their choice is death or the world.   And they do choose.
Earn their brave set of bone, the seeking marvelous look
Of those who lose and use and know their lives.

III

There is a place.   There is a miracle.
I know the nightmare, the black and bone piano,
The statues in the kitchen, a house dissolving in air.
I know the lilac-turreted cathedral
Taking its roots from willows that changed before my eyes
When all became real, real as the sound of bells.
We earthly are aware of transformation;
Miraculously, life, from the old despair.

The wave of smooth water approaches on the sea—
Surface, a live wave individual
Linking, massing its color. Moving, is struck by wind,
Ribbed, steepened, until the slope and ridge begin;
Comes nearer, brightens.   Now curls, its vanishing
Hollows darken and disappear;   now high above
Me, the scroll, froth, foam of the overfall.

IV

Now the ideas all change to animals
Loping and gay, now all the images
Transform to leaves, now all these screens of leaves
Are flowing into rivers, I am in love
With rivers, these changing waters carry voices
Carry all children;   carry all delight.
The water-soothed winds move warm above these waves.
The child changes and moves among these waves.

The waves are changing, they tremble from waves of water
To other essentials — they become waves of light
And wander through my sleep and through my waking.
And through my hands and over my lips and over
Me;   brilliant and transformed and clear,
The pure light.   Now I am light and nothing more.

V

Eating sleep, eating sunlight, eating meat,
Lying in the sun to stare
At deliverance, the rapid cloud,
Gull-wing opposing sun-bright wind,
I see the born who dare
Walk on green, walk against blue,
Move in the nightlong flare
Of love on darkness, traveling
Among the rings of light to simple light,
From nowhere to nowhere.
And in my body feel the seasons grow.
Who is it in the dim room?   Who is there?

VI

Death's threat!   Today I have known laughter
As if for the first time;   have seen into your eyes,
Death, past the still gaze, and found two I love.
One chose you gladly with a laugh advancing,
His hands full of guns, on the enemy in Spain.
The other living with the choice of life
Turning each day of living to the living day.

The strength, the grossness, spirit and gall of choice.
They came to me and said, "If you must choose,
Is it yourself or the child?"   Laughter I learned
In that moment, laughter and choice of life.
I saw an immense ship trembling on the water
Lift by a gesture of hands.   I saw a child.   I saw
A red room, the eyes, the hands, the hands and eyes.

VII

You will enter the world where death by fear and explosion
Is waited;   longed for by many: by all dreamed.
You will enter the world where various poverty
Makes thin the imagination and the bone.
You will enter the world where birth is walled about,
Where years are walled journeys, death a walled-in act.
You will enter the world which eats itself
Naming faith, reason, naming love, truth, fact.

You in your dark lake moving darkly now
Will leave a house that time makes, times to come
Enter the present, where all the deaths and all
The old betrayals have come home again.
World where again Judas, the little child,
May grow and choose.   You will enter the world.

VIII

Child who within me gives me dreams and sleep,
Your sleep, your dreams; you hold me in your flesh
Including me where nothing has included
Until I said : I will include, will wish
And in my belly be a birth, will keep
All delicacy, all delight unclouded.

Dreams of an unborn child move through my dreams,
The sun is not alone in making fire and wave
Find meeting-place, for flesh and future meet
The seal in the green wave like you in me,
Child.   My blood at night full of your dreams,
Sleep coming by day as strong as sun on me,
Coming with sun-dreams where leaves and rivers meet,
And I at last alive sunlight and wave.

IX

Rider of dream, the body as an image
Alone in crisis.   I have seen the wind,
Its tall cloud standing on a pillar of air,
The toe of the whirlwind turning on the ground.
Have known in myself hollow bodiless shade.
The shadow falling from the tree to the ground,
Have lost and lost and now at last am found
For a moment of sleep and waking, striking root.

Praise that the homeless may in their bodies be
A house that time makes, where the future moves
In his dark lake.   Praise that the cities of men,
The fields of men, may at all moments choose.
Lose, use, and live.   And at this daylight, praise
To the grace of the world and time that I may hope
To live, to write, to see my human child.

MARILYN HACKER ON MURIEL RUKEYSER'S
Nine Poems for the unborn child

> Now birth as trauma has an important repressive role in our art
> . . . [in] our literature in particular. Few of the women writing
> poetry have made more than a beginning in writing about birth.
> There is exceptional difficulty in giving form to so crucial a
> group of meanings and experiences.
> —Muriel Rukeyser, "A Simple Theme," *Poetry,* July 1948

Muriel Rukeyser's project was as inclusive as any twentieth-century poet's: her communities of choice were numerous. Her desire was always to open communication between writers/artists/intellectuals, political activists, and working men and women from all walks of life. From her first book, published in 1932 when she was twenty-one, she attempted to analyze the contemporary world through poetry, which, for her, could encompass science, history, popular music, and the new techniques of cinema. Although their politics are opposed, the only other American Modernist poet who demonstrated such a wide reach and such versatility, whose view of the possibilities of poetry was equally generous, was Ezra Pound.

Despite early recognition as a writer, Rukeyser was disinherited by her family in her late twenties for her politics. She had passionate relationships with both men and women. In 1947, she was living and working alone in San Francisco, pregnant by a man whose name she never revealed. In September, her son was born. "Nine Poems for the unborn child" was written during her pregnancy. As far as I know, this sequence is the first to claim for these situations—the physical/mental stages and changes of pregnancy; a single woman's decision to bear and raise a child—the stature of poetic subject matter, neither stigmatized nor sentimentalized at a time when a pregnant single woman in a novel or play would inevitably miscarry, die, or both. (Elizabeth Barrett Browning's verse novel *Aurora Leigh* includes an unmarried mother who doesn't die, but she remains an emblematic, redeemed "ruined maiden," not a protagonist.)

1947: the war, Hiroshima, the Shoah, were as present in Rukeyser's worldview as the events in her body, while the Cold War silenced progressive activists. "Nine Poems" is not a minimalist, domesticated sequence, turning toward the private life in despair or resignation. It posits gestation as a hopeful, chosen antidote to war and repression, in which the conscious woman's mind and body also signify the body politic. Why did Rukeyser compose this poem as a sonnet sequence? The correspondence of pregnancy's discrete "stages" with nine connected but separate poems; the poet's desire to circumnavigate the subject, avoiding rectilinear movement; a dialogue with the form, inscribing a woman's feelings for her unborn child into the "praise of an unattainable beloved" which has historically informed the sonnet sequence: all this may have influenced her choice.

In "Nine Poems," the sonnet's lyrical and narrative possibilities are examined and expanded through Rukeyser's prosodic inventiveness. Architecture and landscapes, human and animal bodies permeate each other—as pregnancy itself is both a state of intense interiority and of engagement in human interdependence. Dichotomies are dismantled: the pregnant poet's body is transformed to "pure light," but darkness is also "promise," the place or state where a new kind of vision becomes possible; ideas become "animals" as the child's presence transcends in corporeal "idea." (A literal-minded reader might wonder if the poet was also referring to the now-superseded rabbit test, in which the creature's demise indicated the presence of new life.)

These are unconventional sonnets. The single woman's learning of and welcoming her pregnancy (embracing an "outlaw" status) is a narrative point of departure. Assonance, consonance, and repetition often stand in for rhyme; the iambic pentameter line sometimes swells to twelve or thirteen syllables, and, more iconoclastically, to six or more stresses. The central, sensual, and contemplative poem V has only twelve lines, while the necessarily narrative II is broken into traditional octave/sestet, with a turn. Rukeyser's sonnets are at once located within the speaker's body and uncontained: "swords" and "fountains" exist both inside and outside her body; "waves" are water, light, the interpenetration of body and mind, of maternal and fetal consciousness, and the transformative power of some outside, benevolent force.

The first half of the twentieth century in the United States saw both Modernist poets and poets who revivified European forms with new subject matter and American vocabulary. There was also a tradition of politically engaged poetry by both black and white women, from Emma Lazarus and Frances Harper in the nineteenth century through Lola Ridge, Kay Boyle, Anne Spencer, Edna St. Vincent Millay, and Genevieve Taggard. Millay's 1929 poem "Menses" might be compared with Rukeyser's in its use of a previously taboo subject as a lens through which to examine human relationships. In "Nine Poems," Rukeyser synthesizes these currents, prefiguring the personal = political equation of second-wave feminism. Having witnessed and written about societal disasters and war, she was uniquely positioned to dare inscribe pregnancy as a human endeavor requiring poetic scrutiny. Her choice of the sonnet sequence was an essential part of that inscription, indicating a continuity. Pregnancy and birth are as much conscious, human experiences as war or amorous longing (and a frequent result of the latter). Poets as disparate as Marie Ponsot, Sylvia Plath, Sharon Olds, Diane DiPrima, and Toi Derricotte have since written about pregnancy and birth: Rukeyser's sequence is their precursor.

February

JAMES SCHUYLER

A chimney, breathing a little smoke.
The sun, I can't see
making a bit of pink
I can't quite see in the blue.
The pink of five tulips
at five P.M. on the day before March first.
The green of the tulip stems and leaves
like something I can't remember,
finding a jack-in-the-pulpit
a long time ago and far away.
Why it was December then
and the sun was on the sea
by the temples we'd gone to see.
One green wave moved in the violet sea
like the UN Building on big evenings,
green and wet
while the sky turns violet.
A few almond trees
had a few flowers, like a few snowflakes
out of the blue looking pink in the light.
A gray hush
in which the boxy trucks roll up Second Avenue
into the sky. They're just
going over the hill.
The green leaves of the tulips on my desk
like grass light on flesh,
and a green-copper steeple
and streaks of cloud beginning to glow.
I can't get over
how it all works in together
like a woman who just came to her window
and stands there filling it
jogging her baby in her arms.

She's so far off. Is it the light
that makes the baby pink?
I can see the little fists
and the rocking-horse motion of her breasts.
It's getting grayer and gold and chilly.
Two dog-size lions face each other
at the corners of a roof.
It's the yellow dust inside the tulips.
It's the shape of a tulip.
It's the water in the drinking glass the tulips are in.
It's a day like any other.

PETER GIZZI ON JAMES SCHUYLER'S February

I love James Schuyler's poetry—its effortlessness and grace, its
sound, its thick and at times gnarly descriptions. A palpable sense of ir-
reality is everywhere present in it. His poems combine the attention of
an ethnographer with the charm of a great dinner guest. Add to this a
private reading of the physical world imprinted on his nervous system.
In his hyper-real descriptions, colors shift; words shimmer. The "violet
sea" verges on the violent, and there's a deeper cold behind the "gold
and chilly" weather.

In one sense, "February" is a painstakingly specific catalog of dis-
crete images. Each line is a surprise, delighting in the pleasures of coin-
cidence, like "the pink of five tulips / at five P.M." Gradually we progress
through the city day to the dust inside the tulip, to the shape of the
tulip, the container the tulip is in (a glass), and the container the glass
is in (this day). The poem draws us from

1) the impalpability of the discrete units of matter; the fuzz of
    memory; the microscopic material of being; the "dust" inside
    the tulip;
2) to the shape of the tulip; its form (seemingly almost a platonic
    form—an ideal form—and yet here it is both symbolic and
    specific);
3) to the container; the context we can "place" it in; the context of
    the day, as the poet records the shifting of the light;

4) to the container of the poem, which can contain more than the day; the poetic tension between the beginning of matter—the baby being jogged on a hip—and the end of matter, the dust we become.

The beauty of the tulip may draw us to observe it, but inside it we see a reflection of what we ourselves are made of, just as we may see an image of our own childhood when we look through someone else's window.

"February" is not a tranquil Romantic recollection; it is active observation that creates the effect of recollection. Schuyler exchanges a syntax of memory and judgment for a syntax of simultaneity. He uncouples his sentences, so that the electric spark must jump from noun to noun and event to event, no matter how disparate. The gaps between his lines give us the experience of the passage of time; they are a kind of verbal time-lapse photography. Schuyler is a watcher. If you look out the window long enough, you can actually "see" time pass as the light and colors of the world shift. In the first poem of his first book, John Ashbery wrote, "Everything has a schedule, if you can find out what it is." One might say that in this poem "February" (the second poem of Schuyler's first book, *Freely Espousing*), he does the work to disclose this invisible schedule, revealing the seemingly random syntax of the physical world.

This world as he presents it is both reassuring and unstable. The "day before March first" is not always February 28, and by not naming it—but naming what is next to it—he draws attention to this hinge of seasonal, temporal change, this "leap." The poem is partly about this passage, getting over the hump of winter, as the truck disappears over the hump of the hill or the speaker "can't get over" his latest observation. In this simple gesture, nature, commerce, and human reason are intertwined. It is this interconnectedness that makes Schuyler's poems reassuring despite the instability of their surface. And yet reality is never as real as it is in a Schuyler poem: one has the sense of events and words being brought together out of necessity, to conduct a vision, giving the apparent randomness of living a sense of coherence and even a symphonic inevitability.

Poem

DELMORE SCHWARTZ

In the morning, when it was raining,
Then the birds were hectic and loudy;
Through all the reign is fall's entertaining;
Their singing was erratic and full of disorder:
They did not remember the summer blue
Or the orange of June. They did not think at all
Of the great red and bursting ball
Of the kingly sun's terror and tempest, blazing,
Once the slanting rain threw over all
The colorless curtains of the ceaseless spontaneous fall.

ROBERT PHILLIPS ON DELMORE SCHWARTZ'S Poem

In a sense, nearly all the poems of Delmore Schwartz (1913–1966) are, by now, lost. Except for a very few famous lyrics—"In the Naked Bed, In Plato's Cave," "The Heavy Bear Who Goes With Me," "The Ballad of the Children of the Czar"—he is rarely anthologized or included in textbooks. He is not, for instance, to be found in Helen Vendler's *Harvard Book of Modern American Poetry,* J. D. McClatchy's *Vintage Book of Contemporary Poetry,* A. Poulin, Jr.'s *Contemporary American Poetry,* or the Academy of American Poets' *Fifty Years of American Poetry.*

So I'm tempted to discuss one of his neglected masterpieces— "The Ballet of the Fifth Year," say, or "Baudelaire," "Seurat's Sunday Afternoon Along the Seine," or "Starlight Like Intuition Pierced the Twelve." Instead, I'll write about one of the poems that literally was overlooked. It never appeared in a book until I gathered it in Schwartz's *Last & Lost Poems* (1979, revised and expanded edition, 1989). It first appeared in *The New York Times* on October 27, 1962, back in the days when that paper published a poem a day on the op-ed page. Schwartz sent several of his last poems there, perhaps for a quick $25 apiece. I remember reading this poem one morning over coffee and being taken by its freshness and vividness.

Schwartz titled it simply "Poem," and when I edited his last poems

I respected his title in such cases, but included the first line in the table of contents for easy identification. It is a very *wet* poem. (Schwartz's later poems often were a riff on a mood or scene or color. In the same posthumous collection, "All Night, All Night" is a very *dark* poem.)

The first two lines of "Poem" are:

In the morning, when it was raining,
Then the birds were hectic and loudy . . .

The third line then posits a typical Schwartz pun:

Through all the reign is fall's entertaining . . .

Puns were an important part of Schwartz's prosody, doubtless a result of his worship of James Joyce's writing. (Schwartz's copy of *Finnegans Wake* was one of the most heavily annotated books I've ever seen. He even named his favorite cat Riverrun.)

Another pun appears in the last line, ". . . the ceaseless spontaneous fall." Here we get, again, the rainfall, but also the autumn. Schwartz used puns the way some poets use enjambment: to create two images at once. And like Joyce, he liked to invent words. The second adjective in the second line, "loudy," does not appear in any dictionary I own, but it is an unusually effective word for the sound of hectic birds. It connotes both loud and rowdy. Another marvelous adjective is "kingly" to describe the sun. Also admirable is the notion of the sun's "terror and tempest, blazing . . ."—an original conceit. "Kingly" also reinforces the earlier noun "reign."

It's a very simple, descriptive nature poem. As is appropriate for a poem on hectic and erratic birdsong, the meter is ragged and the rhyme scheme uneven. We do get raining/entertaining, all/all/ball/fall, but in no given pattern. This is typical of later Schwartz, as opposed to the Schwartz who wrote many sonnets in the late '40s. (He included thirty-seven of them in his 1950 volume *Vaudeville for a Princess*.) His style evolved from formal verse to free verse, from short lines to long lines. His model shifted from Yeats to Whitman. "Poem" is typical of his later, spontaneous effusions, characterized by energy and delight. It was written four years before the poet's premature death. I think it sufficiently demonstrates that, contrary to the opinion of many, Schwartz was writing ingeniously well almost to the end.

[Untitled Poem]

SEIFU

TRANSLATED BY DANIEL C. BUCHANAN

The faces of dolls.
In unavoidable ways
I must have grown old.

COLE SWENSEN ON SEIFU'S Untitled Poem

Like many short poems, this is a very large poem under great pressure. We sense an intricate complex of realization, regret, and reflection, all present and sealed into a single instant. It does not unfold in time, but in space—a presence that radiates in all directions, so that we can't follow it like an argument; we can only feel it, rushing by us at great speed. Ideogrammatic, as Pound would have said, the poem is based on the gap at its center, that void between the two juxtaposed images that is, ultimately, much larger, much more alive than either. The excitement generated by this poem is the vertiginous leap that we make between them, and thus also between the particular and the eternal, between faces and ages.

I first read it when I was eighteen, and I think one of the reasons that it's stuck with me all these years is that it gave me, just for an instant, the actual experience of great age. It was an instant out of the continuum of time, and thus a violation of nature, a second stolen from sixty years hence. It made me stand beside myself.

I don't know much about Seifu, and what I do know is delightfully contradictory. My original source, *One Hundred Famous Haiku* (tr. Daniel C. Buchanan, Japan Publications, 1973), gives her dates as 1650–1721 and tells us that she was a "poetess nun." I enjoyed the order of those labels. The commentary goes on to state that the poem may be a response to Doll Festival Day, and that she realizes that they no longer interest her, which in turn makes her realize she's aging. I couldn't disagree more—I think it's much eerier than that; it's something in the faces themselves, hers and the dolls', some echo in their stillness, some shock of recognition. It's something unnerving, that sensation of being ajar with time.

The one other source I found gave her name as Enomoto Seifu-jo, her dates as 1731–1814, and described her as a student of the haiku poet Shiro of the school of Issa. I'm glad for these differences. I like to think of our Seifu as a doubled personage, an offset of herself spanning almost two hundred years, ajar with time, bridging it with her brush.

The second source included Robert H. Blyth's translation, which reads:

> The faces of the dolls!
> Though I never intended to,
> I have grown old.
> —Seifu-jo

A wonderful poem, but it is not the same poem. Her "unavoidable ways" is so impersonal, so inevitable, so conscious that one's intentions play no part in things. But above all, it lacks the *must* in the final line "I must have grown old." All the surprise—and the acceptance—is there in that word. Of course, neither poem is "right"; a translation is always a collaboration, so just as her history is a double exposure, so is her poem, ajar, with the "real" one perhaps oscillating between. In Japanese, it reads:

> Hina no kao
> Ware zehi naku mo
> Oi ni keri.

For something that happens to so many, so few have captured it; Oppen was another one:

> Old age.
> What a strange thing to happen to a little boy.

Heritage

JAMES STILL

I shall not leave these prisoning hills
Though they topple their barren heads to level earth
And the forests slide uprooted out of the sky.
Though the waters of Troublesome, of Trace Fork,
Of Sand Lick rise in a single body to glean the valleys,
To drown lush pennyroyal, to unravel rail fences;
Though the sun-ball breaks the ridges into dust
And burns its strength into the blistered rock
I cannot leave. I cannot go away.

Being of these hills, being one with the fox
Stealing into the shadows, one with the new-born foal,
The lumbering ox drawing green beech logs to mill,
One with the destined feet of man climbing and descending,
And one with death rising to bloom again, I cannot go.
Being of these hills I cannot pass beyond.

MAGGIE ANDERSON ON JAMES STILL'S Heritage

> This fellow has come over in here from Troublesome Creek and
> settled in the Old Wiley Amburgey house on Dead Mare Branch
> . . . We call him 'the man in the bushes.'
> —a neighbor of James Still, 1939

The range of mountains that makes up the Appalachian region from
Georgia to Maine is 200 million years old, and the physical presence of
these mountains deeply informs the imagination of any writer who has
lived, or whose people have lived, long in this place. "Appalachia is that
somewhat mythical region with no known borders," James Still wrote,
and yet he lived from 1939 until his death at the age of ninety-five in a
two-story log house between Wolfpen Creek and Deadmare Branch, at
the forks of Troublesome Creek in Knott County, Kentucky.

James Still was more widely known as a novelist, the author of the much acclaimed *River of Earth* (Viking Press, 1940), than as a poet; he remains little known at all outside the southern Appalachian region. He published the poem "Heritage" in 1935 in *The New Republic*. Many of his poems and stories appeared in national literary journals in the 1930s and '40s, and then, perhaps because he did not leave the "prisoning hills," Still became classified as a regional writer.

When applied to literary works, the term "regional" is nearly always seen as pejorative, and the writer is often eclipsed by the negative stereotypes of the place from which the deepest sources of the writing come. For those of us from the Appalachian region, the firm ground of our writing—topography, language, history, and music—is misunderstood, appropriated, or otherwise marginalized. James Still understood this well enough. In his later years, he collected stories of the people in his neighborhood in Knott County and published them as *The Wolfpen Notebooks: A Record of Appalachian Life* (1991). In 2001, the University Press of Kentucky published a volume of James Still's new and collected poems, *From the Mountain From the Valley*. He viewed himself as a novelist, children's author, historian, folklorist—and poet. The titles of his poems reflect both his regional affinity and his varied talents: "Fiddlers' Convention on Troublesome Creek," "Night in the Coal Camps," "On Being Drafted into the U.S. Army from My Log Home in March 1942," "After Some Twenty Years Attempting to Describe a Flowering Branch of Redwood," "A Man Singing to Himself," "Fox Hunt on Defeated Creek," and "Those I Want in Heaven with Me Should There Be Such a Place."

The poems of James Still arise from the solid ground of a *place*—what he called the "Earth loved more than any other earth." Still does not merely describe this place but speaks from inside it. He is one with it—"one with the fox / Stealing into the shadows, one with the newborn foal . . ." Nothing—not flood nor drought nor even the toppling of the hills themselves and the uprooting of the forests—can move him from the place of his birthright. There is no separation here between the human and the nonhuman worlds; both are of the hills and so "cannot pass beyond."

"I have gone out to the roads that go up and down," James Still wrote of what we call, in the mountains, "the outside world," a seductive place, gleaming and dangerous, ". . . these wayfares measured with a line / Drawn hard and white from birth to death." When mountain people do leave the hills, they almost always come back, or, as the saying goes, they will die trying. In "White Highways," Still wrote: "I have come back to the long way around, / The far between, the slow arrival." The tension between the inside "homing place" and the outside world is present in all the writings of the Appalachian region. The place itself both cossets and corsets. In "Heritage," the hills are "prisoning" yet the poet "cannot leave. [He] cannot go away." Without this tension, the poem could seem merely a sentimental paean. The negative adjective—and the response to the Biblical injunction which begins the poem—provide its torque. Those, and the language, which hauls itself up like a fiery preacher, "climbing and descending," then pull like a slow sweet fiddle on the heart.

Returning Birds

WISLAWA SZYMBORSKA

TRANSLATED BY STANISLAW BARANCZAK
AND CLARE CAVANAGH

This spring the birds came back again too early.
Rejoice, O reason: instinct can err, too.
It gathers wool, it dozes off—and down they fall
into the snow, into a foolish fate, a death
that doesn't suit their well-wrought throats and splendid claws,
their honest cartilage and conscientious webbing,
the heart's sensible sluice, the entrails' maze,
the nave of ribs, the vertebrae in stunning enfilades,
feathers deserving their own wing in any crafts museum,
the Benedictine patience of the beak.

This is not a dirge—no, it's only indignation.
An angel made of earthbound protein,
a living kite with glands straight from the Song of Songs,
singular in air, without number in the hand,
its tissues tied into a common knot
of place and time, as in an Aristotelian drama
unfolding to the wings' applause,
falls down and lies beside a stone,
which in its own archaic, simpleminded way
sees life as a chain of failed attempts.

ELTON GLASER ON WISLAWA SZYMBORSKA'S Returning Birds

When a poet I've never heard of wins the Nobel Prize in Literature, I prepare myself to be disappointed, always suspicious that considerations other than literary distinction have guided the choice. It was no different when I learned that Wislawa Szymborska had been awarded the honor in 1996. If she were so accomplished, why hadn't I even seen that train wreck of a name before? Hadn't all the worthy poets from Poland, like Czeslaw Milosz and Zbigniew Herbert, already gained international recognition?

But when I tracked down a copy of *View with a Grain of Sand,* Wislawa Szymborska's only collection then available in English translation (by Stanislaw Baranczak and Clare Cavanagh), and began to read the poems, I knew at once that Szymborska was no Swedish mistake. Hers was a mind refreshingly original, expressing itself in poems of unwavering honesty and wry wit. Each page offered a series of quiet astonishments, in lines of understated authority that never felt forced and never took a wrong turn or an easy route to revelation. My only question then was: what godforsaken neck of the woods have I been living in not to have stumbled on such a marvelous poet before?

The poem that confirmed my early excitement was "Returning Birds." Three moments in particular held and amazed me, as they continue to do each time I read the poem. The opening line—"This spring the birds came back again too early"—strikes a neutral tone, with a matter-of-fact statement that sets us up for the next line's more declamatory overturning of complacent opinion: "Rejoice, O reason: instinct can err, too." Isn't that just the opposite of what we'd expect a poet to say? Haven't poets praised the intuitive and the irrational for so long that such celebrations have become rote and tiresome? So the first delight arrives with Szymborska's unconventional response to the tragedy of the birds' miscalculated return.

The second surprise shows up at the end of stanza one, the final item in Szymborska's troped catalogue of the birds' physical effects: "the Benedictine patience of the beak." As good as the other metaphors are, none is as audacious as that one. My own heart's "sensible sluice" surged like a spring freshet when I read that line. Who would have thought to relate a bird's beak to the silent serenity of a monk in the Order of St. Benedict? Did the monk's peaked cowl serve as a visual bridge to get Syzmborska from that monastic order to the bill of a dead bird? It doesn't matter. The connection feels immediately right, and the mind can take its own slow time to work out the logic.

The final thrill appears in the last two lines of the poem. We've been following the downward flight of a bird ambushed by winter, a grounded angel "in an Aristotelian drama," whose body now "lies beside a stone." Then, suddenly, the whole perspective of the poem shifts: we are looking at the world from the stone's point of view, an unyielding refutation of the romantic and the ideal, the progressive and the ameliorative. It's as if that stone made famous as solid proof against Bishop Berkeley's philosophy had learned its lesson only too well at the empirical bottom of Dr. Johnson's boot. What can it do now, "in its archaic, simpleminded way," but "see life as a chain of failed attempts"?

It's one of the mysteries of poetry that such a vision of desolation can feel so exhilarating. Or rather, what we really rejoice in is not that dark view of life—and not reason or instinct, either—but the power of Szymborska's imagination, so free and sweeping that it can bring us down to the level of a dead bird and a bleak stone and, in doing so, lift us beyond ourselves. That is the majesty of all art, to open for us a transcendence we can enter without leaving behind the hard truths of the world. Szymborska achieves this sleight-of-soul again and again. In her poems, she doesn't share the stone's defeated outlook on life. Szymborska never turns her eyes away from the harshness of existence, natural and human, but she also shows us the wonders that lie at our feet or rise, abundantly and inexplicably, all around us.

The Chain Gang Guard

ELEANOR ROSS TAYLOR

The pick strikes differently on the rock
And some resists and some dislodges.
The cars that pass us eye us curiously—
Stodged with our eyes, our frozen triggers cocked.
They move free enough; for them, they're jolly—
The blond one, swinging, sings, "Just like a tree,
Just like a tree, planted by the waters,
I shall not be moved." Easy to see
His spirit's not yet broken. That first chow—
Nose took a squint and stomach shut its eyes;
"I can't eat that," he said. The others spat.
"You may think you can't, but, brother, you lie!"

I don't dare glance to hail the folks I know.
He'll curse or laugh or both as he sees fit,
Cry out to give a stranger's ears a whack,
And throw his hat up for a powdered nose,
Baby oh baby oh baby her,
Die to know where she's off-to up the road.
Playmate, you ain't going nowheres
Unless you want to hear my gun unload.

If I had ever learned to tear-up-jack,
Got drunk enough to leave myself behind,
Could know which time to take and which to pay—
Here I stand! loaded gun across me—
As if I'd get away!

I could choose any poem by Eleanor Ross Taylor for this essay, so seldom is her work anthologized, so little is she known to the (also rare) general reader of poetry. She is not studied in classrooms. *The Norton Anthology* has not noticed her, nor have the writing textbooks full of examples. Taylor is our Emily Dickinson, I believe. If there are readers of serious poetry in the future, they will wonder mightily at our refusal to see her.

Like Dickinson, she is not easy. Like Elizabeth Bishop, she observes closely. Like no one else, she invents an elegant language that is also earthy, southern with a twist. I could choose at random from her first book published in 1960, before anybody could imagine an accomplished southern poet who was native-born and female. I could choose from any of her three spare and widely separated subsequent volumes, including *Late Leisure,* which came out in 1999 from LSU Press. I have chosen an early poem, unusual in that it is spoken in the voice of a man and is more accessible than much of her work. It is nevertheless a representative poem in its presentation of *chosen* captivity, regretted but necessary duty, repressed longing, and the loss of possibility.

The poem is as clear as its title. Its lines are spoken by a man who guards a chain gang, a sight that was common enough on roads maintained by convict labor in an earlier American South. The first lines are seemingly about the rock that is being broken. The pick strikes "differently" and some of the rock "resists" and will not break, and some "dislodges." As life strikes differently, some of us remain firm, whereas some are broken to become other, removed. This expansion is only a hint here and can be intuited only after we have read the thoughts the chain gang guard speaks to himself.

He says, "The cars that pass *us* eye *us* . . ." (emphasis mine), not *them*. Prisoners and guard together make up this "us." The keeper identifies with those he keeps.

In line four comes the peculiar Taylor touch, the unexpected word, a part of elevated or archaic language inserted into everyday speech: "Stodged." *The Oxford English Dictionary* gives *stodge* as a verb of obscure origin, meaning to be filled up, stuffed, surfeited by too much of something. It can also mean to be bogged down, stuck as in mud, slowed by something thick. All these meanings seem to me to glint off the word in this line. The prison group is "stodged" there, stalled, stuck in the given place. They are filled with a surfeit of staring, both the staring they do and the staring back done by the passers-by. The chain gang is stodged there with eyes and triggers *cocked.* Passers-by, too, are stodged with staring, slowed. Surely these two lines, with their curious construction and the heavy, archaic word, take on a number of slant meanings. The cocked triggers are "frozen," a phrasing that carries overtones of power stalled, of sexuality stalled. The prisoners have triggers too, inside them, included as they are in this "us."

In line five, the prisoners become "they" as the guard speaks of them as separate, different from himself. He says they move quite freely on the work gang, and are even jolly, "for them." A young blond man is singled out for comment in the next lines, he who is singing the stalwart hymn about not being moved. This is a new prisoner, his spirit intact. Enter here Taylor's characteristic dead-on use of country talk. The guard remembers or imagines this new prisoner at his first meal: "Nose took a squint" and "stomach shut its eyes"—though the second metaphor seems awkward, it is redeemed by the first, and by the humor. The new prisoner is told by the others that he *will* indeed eat the awful food he has at first refused, that he will be forced to do whatever is required for survival. The tone here implies that the guard feels a certain pleasure in the prisoner's discomfort.

In the first line of stanza two, the guard moves from his thoughts about the new prisoner to his own situation. He, the guard, the "cock" of this walk, actually doesn't dare to act in the presence of those he guards. He can't hail passers-by he knows lest the young prisoner yell something inappropriate or laugh at the guard. Yet the prisoner notices passing women with free expressions of his sexual appreciation of them. The thought of this angers the guard into remembering who's in charge here. "You ain't going nowheres" says the man with the gun, trying for power.

Then comes the pensive final stanza, the one with the surprise of utter simplicity. The colloquial "tear-up-jack" makes it more poignant. The guard begins to wish he'd had some of what the prisoners own, the freedom to transgress, to know "which time to take and which to pay." They, at least, have *taken* for themselves something, some time that was theirs utterly, however criminally spent, however paid for in jail time. The guard, on the other hand, has dared nothing. He cannot "leave himself behind."

> Here I stand! loaded gun across me—
> As if I'd get away!

The loaded gun "across me" becomes, instead of a demonstration of power, an image of a restraint across the body.

The poem is about freedom denied, and it plays with *which freedom? whose freedom?* throughout. No one wins here. The prisoners are restrained by their chains, their circumstance, the acts of their past lives, yet they express open sexuality, hilarity, inappropriate loudness. They can break the rules of puritan propriety and class any time they want, caught though they are. Yet the poem is not really about them. It is about the rock that resists, the celebration denied, the sexuality repressed, the longing that even power can't soften.

With a sly simplicity and slightly torqued language—in other poems Taylor can make syntax dance the fantastic—and with moments of entirely natural speech, the poet uses formal elements that include her usual and highly original slant rhyming. She moves the poem through hint after hint, in ambiguity and humor, steadily toward the perfect final stanza. That last line with its showy rhyme completes the alterations of tone that have formed the arc of the poem. That last line finishes with a knowing surrender, suppressed anger, a wry stasis.

Originally published in Taylor's first book in 1960, when the poet was forty years old, this poem is like others in that collection so wonderfully titled *Wilderness of Ladies*. It can be first one thing and then another. Turn it one way, and it's a light treatise on the nature of freedom; turned another, it's a lyric with a narrative inside; turned again, it just might be a witty comment in code on the experience of woman. Women dared not transgress. They were, especially in the South, the keepers not only of home and family but also virtue and civility. In the context of Taylor's other poems, many of which are spoken in the voices of the almost-voiceless white women of an earlier rural South, this poem is subtler than it seems.

Water Lilies

SARA TEASDALE

If you have forgotten water lilies floating
On a dark lake among mountains in the afternoon shade,
If you have forgotten their wet, sleepy fragrance,
Then you can return and not be afraid.

But if you remember, then turn away forever
to the plains and the prairies where pools are far apart.
Then you will not come at dusk on closing water lilies,
and the shadow of mountains will not fall on your heart.

ANNIE FINCH ON SARA TEASDALE'S Water Lilies

Like a classic haiku, Sara Teasdale's "Water Lilies" is distinguished by a restraint which opens overlapping meanings. The sight of the water lilies, their scent, the shadow of the mountains could all mean so many things: a remembered encounter, a secret, perhaps an erotic experience, maybe a female-centered one, perhaps none of this.

The poem keeps such profound boundaries that its very secrecy gives rise to a disarming clarity and openness. The inexorably falling beat, alternating between heavily and lightly stressed trochees in the second line, adds to a sureness of tone that suggests a private visionary experience. What happened in those mountains? What was so intimate it can never be named, yet so universal that the poet is addressing all of us about it? Or is she addressing only one person? Then what would it mean if I were somehow that one person? Or you?

I find Teasdale cooler, sadder, more polished than the more well-known Edna St. Vincent Millay. She is like a secret, and holds something of the same quality I love in Dickinson: her own strong center of gravity, her own counsel to keep. Although Teasdale and Millay both write of erotic and often painful experience, Millay seems certain of having a sympathetic audience. What draws me to Teasdale is her intense self-sufficiency, her privacy. When I have shown her magnetic, self-contained poems to friends of all levels of education, they love her. Like Frost, Teasale works for many types of readers without seeming to try.

It would have made sense for my mother, who taught me so much about poetry, to introduce me to Teasdale, but she didn't. Millay was the poet she had grown up on—and raised me on when my father wasn't looking. Nor did I come to know Teasdale because of my frequent childhood visits with my parents to the house of Teasdale's editor, the poet Marya Zaturenska, and her husband, the poet Horace Gregory. Out of all that blend of talk about publishers and Pulitzers and the relative ranks of great and lesser poets, I recall mainly Marya's strange left arm, bloated with gout; Horace's kind voice; dusty wine glasses; and the impressive library of poetry on the tiny top floor of the house. Not Teasdale. Teasdale was my own discovery.

"Water Lilies" was a discovery I made out of self-defense, when I was in graduate school in creative writing in 1985. No one I knew there had read Teasdale, and everyone was dead certain there was no reason to. I knew that somewhere was a poem of hers that even those whose knees jerked hard at anything "sentimental" (which in many cases could be translated to mean "anything too blatantly female") would appreciate. One evening, I browsed through her *Collected Poems* with a mission. Though I was drawn to the passionate, emotionally open lyrics such as "She Who Could Bind You" and "Like Barley Bending," now I passed over anything that explicitly mentioned love, death, or the word "I." When I came to "Water Lilies," I knew I had found what I was looking for. I brought it in to the graduate workshop the next day, and when the poet in charge, Edward Hirsch, read it, he drew in his breath, nodded, said he was surprised, and never said anything dismissive about Teasdale to me again.

Some years later, in the winter of 1990, I found myself schlepping my six-week old son through the Modern Language Association annual convention book fair. By the time I passed the Feminist Press table, he had grown fussy and hungry and I was stuffing him under my jacket, trying to nurse him as I walked: high time for a break, and Feminist Press had an empty and inviting-looking chair. I struck up a conversation with the director, Florence Howe, who told me she was putting the final touches on a revised and more comprehensive edition of her classic anthology of American women's poetry, *No More Masks*.

"Is Teasdale in it?" was my first question. "No," said Florence in surprise, "it never occurred to me to put *her* in." I had used up my shocked dismay in the mid-1980s, when Gilbert and Gubar had left Teasdale entirely out of their encyclopedic *Norton Anthology of Women's Poetry,* so I kept my head. Here was my chance. "Is Teasdale really any good?" Florence was asking. "I'll send you a poem or two," I told her, thinking, with grateful confidence, of "Water Lilies."

So I sent her two photocopied pages on which I had circled "Water Lilies" and one other poem, also carefully screened for sentiment. And then it was Florence's turn to surprise me. When the new *No More Masks* came out, she had included not only my two circled poems but also every single other poem that had been on those poems' facing pages in my muddy reprint of the 1930s edition of the *Collected Poems of Sara Teasdale.* Florence was a fan, and "Water Lilies" was not alone any longer. But it is still my Teasdale talisman.

The Cat and the Sea

R. S. THOMAS

It is a matter of a black cat
On a bare cliff top in March
Whose eyes anticipate
The gorse petals;

The formal equation of
A domestic purr
With the cold interiors
Of the sea's mirror.

I suspect that our attractions to poems are quite a bit like our attractions to people—seemingly superficial. We like something about the surface first—looks, certain expectations linked to the initial impression—but as we get to know person or poem, we feel connections we wouldn't immediately have guessed. One of my poet-friends is drawn to "skinny" poems and lanky baseball players, but neither would interest her for long unless they turned out to have other virtues. A man across the room catches my eye. Something about the way he's dressed or a gesture he makes with his hands says *home* or *family* or possibly the opposite—*exotic other*—whatever the unconscious responds to before we can articulate it (assuming we ever can). Sometimes a stranger's face looks so open I think the person is easily knowable, but I'm usually wrong. Few people are entirely uncomplicated, just as few poems are. I can't recall what first drew me to R. S. Thomas' "The Cat and the Sea," or even when, but I can make some guesses.

First, the compactness of the poem gives the impression of accessibility. Of course, I know better. Anyone who has grappled with Emily Dickinson's dense elusiveness would think twice before equating small with easy. I had surely read Dickinson long before I encountered Thomas. Still, the way a poem appears on the page does affect my interest in reading it. My own early poems tended to be brief, so I was probably on the lookout for models, poems that did in the space of a few lines all that I hoped to do in my own. In the case of "The Cat and the Sea," my assumption of an effortless entrance into the poem turns out to be true. Richness and complexity are there in abundance, but not at the expense of clarity. And what an intriguing title, with its suggestion of nursery rhyme or fairy tale.

Who could resist a first line like "It is a matter of a black cat?" My ear takes a childlike pleasure in the repetition of sounds—here the *a* sound in *matter, black,* and *cat,* with *black's* "b" picked up in the next line by *bare.* And then, suddenly, whatever nursery-rhyme connection there might have been almost disappears. I'm with the cat on a bare cliff top in March, where the wind cuts into my skin. I know that kind of cold all too well, real and metaphoric. And the cat is *anticipating* something mysterious. Gorse petals. The word *gorse* feels good on the tongue, and its sound suggests something faintly gothic. The American equivalent of *gorse* is *juniper.* Does a cat eat juniper petals? Or maybe it's not thinking of food at all. Maybe (more fancifully) this cat anticipates *seeing* the gorse petals. Maybe it has an aesthetic sense that recognizes gorse petals as beautiful! The dictionary tells me that *gorse* is also an Old English word for *horror,* an etymology surely not lost on the poet.

The genius of this poem is its ability to evoke so many things, almost simultaneously, with such economy. We have the cat's multiple nature (domestic, intelligent, sensitive, potentially malign), and its suggested corollary to humans. What is brief animal life to the indifferent universe, with its ability to swallow us whole without leaving a ripple? The poem's brevity, deceptively light manner, and dark turn make me think of Robert Frost's "Fire and Ice" and "Nothing Gold Can Stay," two other early favorites of mine.

R. S. Thomas is a Welsh Anglican priest whose religious unorthodoxy echoes my own. He is willing to confront our terror of death and to make art from the "formal equation" of ordinary living, the "domestic purr" that reassures, with the knowledge that our end is always before us, that we see ourselves reflected in that chilly knowledge. The slant rhyme of *purr* and *mirror* reinforces the "formal equation," but without the too-neat closure a full rhyme could suggest.

So everything is here. Beauty and fear lie down together, like the lion and the lamb, embedded in surprisingly simple language. And the poem puts a formal frame around experience, giving me a momentary illusion of control over frightening experience, even as it reminds me of what I would prefer to forget. I can imagine Frost smiling over this little poem, seeing in it what Thomas must have learned from him—things I would like to believe I learned from them both.

The Ruiner of Lives

CHASE TWICHELL

Who knows how things end up
spliced together in the mind.

Last night the car was lugging
up the long hill toward home
when a fox came sleepwalking

out of the alders onto the road.
Something was wrong with it.
It listed a little to one side

and moved without fox-quickness,
not sniffing, not scared,
but calm, almost formal,

with a yellow opacity in its eyes

as if it had recently
been dreaming of being blind.

It stood staring down the double barrel
of the headlights till I stopped the car.

Who knows why, but at that moment
five words came awake in my mind:

God the ruiner of lives—

A line of graffiti I once saw
sprayed on a pink wall in the tropics.
Now five sharp stars in a northern night,
shaken out of their sleep.

It was only August, but already
the uppermost leaves of the stricken maples
were ragged and red,

and the small curled leaves
of the barren apples
skittered across the road.

The fox and I—who was our ruiner?

I with the sin of despair
for the world my species has spoiled,

the fox with its hunger,
its rabies, its dirty coat
slung over a frail skeleton.

A fox of the future
digging in the underbrush
for our remains will find

more trash than bones.

I laid my hand over my heart
to put out the fire lit by this idea,
and stroked and stroked as if it were

a terrorist I could cure of its rage
with kindness and animal calm.

The yellow eyes went on dreaming
the car, the road curved into the dark.

Poor fox, poor mystic,
attracted to a light it can't explain.

A light that drives away,
and leaves us both
here under the cold,

crumbling trees of heaven.

C. K. WILLIAMS ON CHASE TWICHELL'S The Ruiner of Lives

I certainly wouldn't describe Chase Twichell's work as lost, since so many lovers of poetry admire her work; it would be better to say that "The Ruiner of Lives" is one of those poems which is inadequately attended to. A poem can be a thousand years or a month old and fit that category; it is one of those poems one would like to have inscribed on the walls of the mind, to have in one's awareness all the time.

"The Ruiner of Lives" has been with me since I first read it. The sadness of it, the wisdom, the vision, the poetic force. And the fox, that fox, unlike any other animal in our literature, always utterly singular, yet in a constant process of transfiguration. It is a fox that sleepwalks like a human and lists like a ship, that enters onto the stage of our attention like a dancer and departs as a once-beautiful vixen-woman, with her own filthy coat slung over her shoulder as she staggers out into a cosmic homelessness. The fox regards us with the opacity of psychosis and dreams of itself as once only humans could, dreams the terrible dementia of its rabies as a kind of blindness, though it sees, more clearly than we do, how we remain intruders in the world of nature which we violate, how even the lights of our cars are weapons of death, and how even our lives on this planet have become, in many ways, weapons of death as well.

Often with me, too, is the voice of the poem, which moves through so many tonalities, so many chromatics. It is a voice that wonders about itself and tragically abstracts from itself, that quests and reflects and transforms, that grieves and regrets, that rues the limits of its powers of knowing and rues as well the sin of despair, which renders it impotent even to try to effect the reformation of our species, the reconfiguration of our common soul, which might compel us to see what we are wreaking under the crumbling trees of heaven.

And the god in the poem, potent, but only to devise ruin, and the heart in the poem, which is a terrorist, which might be calmed by our self-stroking, but won't be, and which might be redeemed, if there were a metaphor stupendous enough to undertake such a task. Because, the poems tells us, to change ourselves really we would have to submit to something as thorough as the sick mysticism of the fox, whose soul in yet another transformation is a moth drawn towards a hallucinated light: all that remains of a vision of a god who might possibly not be a destroyer.

I read this poem and I see, I think, I opine, I conclude, I hope, I grieve, I am called to and driven away, and, as I say, for no reason I can understand, I am exalted, transfigured myself, even though it is a poem of such vast, tragic desolation. How can that be? And why is it that I always rush, though I know the poem well, from one line to the next, as though I had never read a word of it before, as though my life depended on finally reading it now? Why is my familiarity repeatedly and blessedly betrayed, so as I read it I feel as though I'd never read not only this poem but, for that moment, any poem, ever? I follow as this poem leaps first towards its own mind, to wonder how disparate realities can be adjoined there, then out to the world, the fox, alders, to that horrid and harrowing accurate phrase that spikes god, or our sad conception of god, to the mind, to a wall, to the coldest night. Then maples, barren apples; then world, world, world, violated, despoiled, and the spirit thrown back to that single inconsequential beast who soon will lie rotting in the earth, just as we will, though we will be invisible, incoherent, in the vile stuff of our leavings.

A poem of the intensities of the mind, of our astounding ability to transfigure matter to spirit, yet, because humans never sufficiently appreciate the responsibilities which the gift of consciousness entails, also of our dreadful capacity to destroy both. A poem, though, too, which has its place in the heart, because the heart ever hopes, after all the rest, that its frustration and rage might be redeemed by so much resolving passion.

Summer Has Come

AUTHOR UNKNOWN

TRANSLATED BY KUNO MEYER

Summer has come, healthy and free,
Whence the brown wood is bent to the ground:
The slender nimble deer leap,
And the path of seals is smooth.

The cuckoo sings gentle music,
Whence there is smooth peaceful calm:
Gentle birds skip upon the hill,
And swift grey stags.

Heat has laid hold of the rest of the deer—
The lovely cry of curly packs!
The white extent of the strand smiles,
There the swift sea is roused.

A sound of playful breezes in the tops
Of a black oakwood is Drum Daill,
The noble hornless herd runs,
To whom Cuan-wood is a shelter.

Green bursts out on every herb,
The top of the green oakwood is bushy,
Summer has come, winter has gone,
Twisted hollies wound the hound.

The blackbird sings a loud strain,
To him the live wood is a heritage,
The sad angry sea is fallen asleep,
The speckled salmon leaps.

The sun smiles over every land,
A parting for me from the brood of cares:
Hounds bark, stags tryst,
Ravens flourish, summer has come!

On my sixteenth birthday, my sister Susan gave me a copy of *A Little Treasury of World Poetry,* edited by Hubert Creekmore. A pale blue hardcover with a yellow spine, and smaller than most books, it was always in a bag I carried or beside my bed. It was published in 1952 and in the back of it are black-and-white photos, on slick paper, of many of the poets. I read it from cover to cover.

It was an anonymous Celtic poem translated by Kuno Meyer, more than any of those named and enlivened by a face, which literally changed me. In the poem "Summer Has Come" I first felt the necessity of poetry. As Robin Flower, in his book *The Irish Tradition,* writes of the poets of early Ireland: "These scribes and anchorites lived by the destiny of their dedication in an environment of wood and sea; it was because they brought into that environment an eye washed miraculously clear by a continual spiritual exercise that they, first in Europe, had that strange vision of natural things in an almost unnatural purity."

It is a poetry of awakened consciousness set free by discipline, by the laboring body. The poem is free of attributes and only the names of places evoke a particular nostalgia. These names prove that someone is there, behind the poem, while the words and images are like darts and thorns that pierce the air itself. I love the way no natural thing is violated by an idea or a personality in this poem. This is poverty of spirit proved in words.

[There was a man of double deed]

UNKNOWN

There was a man of double deed,
Who sowed his garden full of seed;
When the seed began to grow,
'Twas like a garden full of snow;
When the snow began to melt,
'Twas like a ship without a belt;
When the ship began to sail,
'Twas like a bird without a tail;
When the bird began to fly,
'Twas like an eagle in the sky;
When the sky began to roar,
'Twas like a lion at my door;
When my door began to crack,
'Twas like a stick across my back;
When my back began to smart,
'Twas like a penknife in my heart;
And when my heart began to bleed,
'Twas death, and death, and death indeed.

TOI DERRICOTTE ON [There was a man of double deed]

When I took my first poetry workshop in New York in 1968, my poetry teacher, Pearl London, assigned X. J. Kennedy's *An Introduction to Poetry.* She read a poem aloud to us one afternoon in order to show us the power of rhyme. The first line caught me with its hypnotic rhythm and enigmatic meaning: "There was a man of double deed." Who was the mysterious man of double deed, and what were the twin deeds he was doing? I loved how the poem catapulted the reader into one mysterious world after another. I didn't know where I was going to emerge, yet I kept thinking that, in some way, the poet was leading me toward the solution. Since then, I have read that poem to hundreds of my poetry students, from kindergarteners to graduate students, and they have all been captivated.

A fourth grader once explained the meaning of the poem to me: The man of double deed is every man, he said. We all plant our seeds, the seeds grow, the garden gets bigger, our life turns and twists and changes, and it seems we are out in the big wide world, soaring free. Then something happens. We realize that there is a danger approaching. The man who plants the seed of life is also planting his death.

I have used this poem to teach students that they have a natural gift for poetry. I do this because so many people, adults and children alike, think they don't know anything about poetry and that the teacher is going to end up by telling them they are stupid. So the first day of class, before I even introduce myself, I stand very still at the front of the room until I get their attention, and then I start that poem, speaking it by heart. I know how the students will jump in their skins when, at the end of the poem, the word "a" changes to "my," pointing to our own inescapable and fast-approaching fate.

After I've finished reciting, I say, "O.K. Now you do it." They look at me blankly. "Do what?" "You say it," I say. "We don't know it," they exclaim. That's when I change them into possible poets and lovers of poetry. "You can do it," I say. "Don't worry." And then they start.

"There Was a Man of Double Deed" proves that when a great poem catches you up, you don't even know that your brain and heart are learning intensely. Sure enough, almost everyone can recite the poem by heart. At a certain point, after they work up a little confidence, say by the time the snow begins to melt, I can even stop saying it with them. I close my mouth and stand there the way the magician takes away her hand from the body floating in the middle of the air.

Distraction

HENRY VAUGHAN

O knit me, that am crumbled dust! The heap
     Is all dispersed and cheap;
      Give for a handful, but a thought
        And it is bought;
          Hadst thou
Made me a star, a pearl, or a rainbow,
      The beams I then had shot
      My light had lessened not,
        But now
I find myself the less, the more I grow;
      The world
Is full of voices; Man is called and hurled
      By each, he answers all,
      Knows ev'ry note and call,
        Hence, still
Fresh dotage tempts, or old usurps his will.
Yet, hadst thou clipped my wings, when coffined in
     This quickened mass of sin,
      And saved that light, which freely thou
        Didst then bestow,
        I fear
I should have spurned, and said thou didst forbear;
      Or that thy store was less,
      But now since thou didst bless
        So much,
I grieve, my God! that thou hast made me such.
        I grieve?
O, yes! thou know'st I do; come, and relieve
     And tame, and keep down with thy light
     Dust that would rise, and dim my sight,
      Lest left alone too long
      Amidst the noise and throng,
        Oppressèd I
Striving to save the whole, by parcels die.

More than 300 years ago, Welshman Henry Vaughan practiced med-
icine in a country village, dabbled in alchemy, and wrote the poems that
we continue to read today. Why do his words touch us? Perhaps it's his
heightened alertness to the particulars of the natural world. Perhaps we
love the intimate voice that cries out across generations "O knit me, that
am crumbled dust!" Perhaps it is simply the odd leaps and turns of his
mind. I came to Henry Vaughan's poems via George Herbert, Vaughan's
near-contemporary. Where Herbert is earnest, Vaughan is playful. And
where Herbert takes pains with the logic of his poetic constructions,
Vaughan is not nearly so neat. Indeed, he is fresh, even strange.

In "Distraction," Vaughan gives us one installment in a sustained
spiritual autobiography. He grieves over his faith; he laments his human
weaknesses. In this regard, he is similar to other Metaphysical poets of
the seventeenth century, such as George Herbert, John Donne, Thomas
Traherne, and Richard Crashaw. Each struggled with sin and redemp-
tion and did so with stylistic wit and energy. But Vaughan's character-
istic intensity, his contemplative passion, and eccentric imagery remind
me that he may have more in common with the other bards of weird-
ness: William Blake, John Clare, Gerard Manley Hopkins, and fellow
Welshman Dylan Thomas.

Visionary poets need a welcoming and receptive audience—readers
willing, sometimes, to forgo logical transition and measured argument.
Passionate poetry can be messy, and "Distraction" has some momen-
tary lapses in logic. Certainly, skeptics or ironists will not find much to
admire in Vaughan. Like his American contemporary, Edward Taylor,
Vaughan often veers rather than coheres. But that's fine with me. I am
engaged by his instantaneous perceptions. I like the way his tone shifts
from anguish, at the start of the poem, to the simple gravity of the
middle section, in the lines "The world / Is full of voices; Man is called
and hurled/ By each . . ." Vaughan likes to break into plain talk after art-
ful music; his are the kinds of abrupt and energetic shifts in tone I have
come to love. I do not forget that Vaughan has borrowed many of these
strategies from Herbert, his literary mentor and model. In the poems of
both, a situation can turn unexpectedly, and poof! all is changed, a ter-
rible beauty born.

In addition to being doctor and poet, Henry Vaughan was also a twin. His brother Thomas was a well-known alchemist and hermetic philosopher, urbane and engaged where Vaughan was reclusive and countrified. After Thomas' early death, Vaughan wrote the poems collected in the two-volume *Silex Scintillans*, his most intense and accomplished collection. These poems repeatedly suggest a connection between alchemical transformation and Vaughan's own knowledge of medicine and the body's affairs. His brother's alchemy provides a fruitful metaphor for Vaughan.

In "Distraction," the body morphs from one thing to another, dissolving, alchemically transforming. Alchemy has traditionally been linked with the effort to turn base metals into gold. Several of Vaughan's poems reverse this notion, so that gold becomes lead, a thing of value suddenly devolving. In "Distraction," the disintegration of the body suggests a parallel dissolution of the soul. The poem opens with a call for help ("O knit me"). Like other Metaphysical poets, he speaks directly to his God. And in seeking answers, he uncovers his own insubstantial self: he dissolves to dust, he is "dispersed" and made "cheap." No alchemical cure here. Instead, Vaughan's bodily and spiritual shape-shifting suggest that his redemption won't take place without self-criticism and intense self-scrutiny.

"Distraction" may not be so much a lost poem as one simply overshadowed by Vaughan's more anthologized verses. What is the fate of the poetry of the past? Poets send into the future a few signature poems by which they are recognized. Think T. S. Eliot and see if *The Waste Land* or "The Love Song of J. Alfred Prufrock" doesn't pop into your head. Do the same with Elizabeth Bishop and "One Art" or "In the Waiting Room." This isn't a bad thing. But it is like listening to greatest-hits albums. Soon we forget that there are other poems to pay attention to. If we have read Vaughan at all, we would most likely have found the readily available "They Are All Gone into the World of Light" or "Regeneration." These are wonderful, of course. But some anthologies flatten the experience of reading poetry by only teaching us how groups of poets belong to their literary period. What do we miss? A full accounting of the individual voices emerging from that time. I'd rather not partake of only a part of Vaughan. I want him whole and complete, oddities and all.

Making Love to Myself

JAMES L. WHITE

When I do it, I remember how it was with us.
Then my hands remember too,
and you're with me again, just the way it was.

After work when you'd come in and
turn the TV off and sit on the edge of the bed,
filling the room with gasoline smell from your overalls,
trying not to wake me which you always did.
I'd breathe out long and say,
'Hi Jess, you tired baby?'
you'd say not so bad and rub my belly,
not after me really, just being sweet,
and I always thought I'd die a little
because you smelt like burnt leaves or woodsmoke.

We were poor as Job's turkey but we lived well—
the food, a few good movies, good dope, lots of talk,
lots of you and me trying on each other's skin.

What a sweet gift this is,
done with my memory, my cock and hands.

Sometimes I'd wake up wondering if I should fix
coffee for us before work,
almost thinking you're here again, almost seeing
your work jacket on the chair.

I wonder if you remember what
we promised when you took the job in Laramie?
Our way of staying with each other.
We promised there'd always be times
when the sky was perfectly lucid,
that we could remember each other through that.

You could remember me at my worktable
or in the all-night diners,
though we'd never call or write.

I just have to stop here Jess.
I just have to stop.

DAVID WOJAHN ON Making Love to Myself

This poem is a masturbatory fantasy. It is also a kind of ars poetica and a wise and affecting examination of the function of memory. It appears in *The Salt Ecstasies,* a posthumously published collection by the Minnesota poet James L. White, and it strikes me as one of his most representative poems. I often go back to White's poetry, for its virtues remain instructive. The emotional directness and abject plainness of White's verse reminds me that, contrary to what Oscar Wilde said, good writing can be sincere, especially during an era when too many of my generational peers have lost themselves in a poetry of dissonance and intellectual sophistry. White's poetry has spoken to others in this way, for *The Salt Ecstasies* has found a small but fervent readership over the years.

The poets that most influenced White were C. P. Cavafy and James Wright. From Cavafy, White developed a style that was skeptical of metaphor and unafraid of statement. And like Cavafy, White was a gay writer whose unabashed out-ness was unusual for his time. Via Wright, White arrived at a vernacular style of deceptive simplicity. Thanks in part to its ease with demotic speech, the poem maintains a tone of casual intimacy that allows it to make a number of abrupt tonal shifts; the consolation of nostalgia repeatedly gives way to a more acute sense of loss. "Making Love to Myself" is so bald, so emotionally unguarded, that the poem shouldn't work at all. And yet it seems to me deeply resonant.

The plainness of White's delivery, with its uncomplicated syntax and absence of enjambment, is deceptive: it is by no means artless. The minimalism of White's manner allows him to make a seamless shift between the fantasy that initiates the poem and the recollections that arrive in stanza two. White evokes the couple's relationship with a spare precision—"you'd come in and / turn the TV off and sit on the edge of the bed, / filling the room with the gasoline smell of your overalls"; "You'd . . . rub my belly, / not after me really, just being sweet."

Lest we forget, however, that the poem is about "making love to myself," White then offers the single-sentence aside that comprises the fourth stanza: "What a sweet gift this is, / done with my memory, my cock and hands." Surely this is not the first time someone has equated the process of writing a lyric poem with autoeroticism, but here both are seen as a kind of delivery system for memory, and the pathos and urgency of White's aside deepens the impact of the memories that follow. The demise of the couple's relationship is sketched with crisp attentiveness.

The ending of the poem is its most compelling moment, and its resistance to familiar means of closure surprises us not through its artifice but through its candor. We don't know if the speaker is ending the poem because he is emotionally overwhelmed by his recollections or if he is experiencing some post-orgasmic *triste*. Both explanations are plausible, but both are also needlessly reductive; this is a haunted poem, and the ending works as good closures should, completing the poem on narrative, thematic, and rhetorical terms while at the same time remaining mysterious.

If you read and write poetry long enough, you carry around inside your head a small anthology of the poems you can't imagine living without. For me, "Making Love to Myself" is one of those poems. And the place it occupies in my personal anthology is a secure one. Such collections have little to do with hierarchies or canons. I'd rather have White's poem in my table of contents than I would a whole host of poems by more "important" poets. This is to say that I will continue to learn from this poem, from its candor as well as its unobtrusive formal grace.

Time to Come

WALT WHITMAN

O, Death! a black and pierceless pall
    Hangs round thee, and the future state;
No eye may see, no mind may grasp
    That mystery of fate.

This brain, which now alternate throbs
    With swelling hope and gloomy fear;
This heart, with all the changing hues,
    That mortal passions bear—

This curious frame of human mould,
    Where unrequited cravings play,
This brain, and heart, and wondrous form
    Must all alike decay.

The leaping blood will stop its flow;
    The hoarse death-struggle pass; the cheek
Lay bloomless, and the liquid tongue
    Will then forget to speak.

The grave will tame me; earth will close
    O'er cold dull limbs and ashy face;
But where, O, Nature, where shall be
    The soul's abiding place?

Will it e'en live? For though its light
    Must shine till from the body torn;
Then, when the oil of life is spent,
    Still shall the taper burn?

O, powerless is this struggling brain
    To rend the mighty mystery;
In dark, uncertain awe it waits
    The common doom, to die.

On July 6, 1855, the first advertisement appeared in the New York *Tribune* for the slender green book that changed the course of American poetry. Two dollars was a fair price for the first edition of *Leaves of Grass.* Walt Whitman intended to make his book available on July 4, but the bookstores were closed that day.

It is impossible now to measure the newness of those first twelve untitled poems—the sprawling free-verse lines, the cocksure optimism of his "democratic" voice, and the idiom, which fused street lingo and operatic grandeur with religious conviction and erotic candor. Ralph Waldo Emerson recognized his brilliance immediately. His letter to Whitman, written on July 21, famously "greet[s Whitman] at the beginning of a great career." Whitman carried the letter in his pocket all summer. If *Leaves* seemed to spring out of thin air, still Emerson shrewdly guessed that it "must have had a long foreground somewhere."

Critics commonly mark the beginning of Whitman's poetic career in 1855. Whitman himself encouraged such a notion, suggesting in "Song of Myself" that "I, now thirty-seven years old in perfect health begin." (This line doesn't appear until the 1881 edition of *Leaves of Grass,* published when Whitman was sixty-two.) But Emerson correctly assumed the long preparation. By the late 1830s, still in his teens, Whitman was writing hard, and through the 1840s he published many poems, two dozen short stories, a novel, as well as dozens—perhaps hundreds—of sketches and editorials for New England newspapers and magazines.

Whitman's first published poem appeared unsigned on October 31, 1838, in the *Long Island Democrat.* "Our Future Lot" is the work of a talented teenager, conventional in taste and form, whose speaker mines the traditional gloom and melodrama of the period's magazine verse. Appearing in *Aurora* on April 9, 1842 and written by "Walter Whitman," "Time to Come" is a substantially revised version of "Our Future Lot."

I don't claim that "Time to Come" is a great poem. Rather, it is a fascinating early poem by a great poet. Few know it; fewer have examined it. Between the appearance in 1838 of "Our Future Lot" and *Leaves of Grass* in 1855, Whitman himself evolved: from failed teacher to journeyman printer to editor to poet; from shy teenager to foppish Brooklyn dandy to "one of the roughs," complete with open-collared, broadcloth shirts and undomesticated beard. Likewise, "Time to Come" falls midway between his sentimental earliest poems and the audaciously original *Leaves of Grass*. It foreshadows some of Whitman's greatest later themes while still demonstrating residuals from his earliest work.

"Time to Come" will strike new readers for its conventional poetics. We are just not prepared to hear rhyme and meter from Whitman, our first great free-verse poet. His rhymes are obvious but (at least) not forced. In fact, their frequent ideational juxtapositions show a sophisticated wit. The physicality of "state" is ironized by the abstractness of "Fate"; one must "bear" the "fear" of obliteration; the body's "play" inevitably must "decay," and so forth. The final quatrain's rhyme of "mystery" and "die" is the poem's most distant and unbalanced rhyme, and that final, fatal infinitive seems effectively to bite off any further development of the narrative.

Whitman's iambic rhythm is traditional and, occasionally, graceful. Notice how each stanza's fourth line—trimeter rather than tetrameter—serves to emphasize the shortened life of the stanza, thus marrying form and content. For such a conventional poem, "Time to Come" features a number of well-enjambed lines, as in stanza four. Whitman's extended syntax unfolds with poise, though he clearly does get tangled in the sixth stanza. Here, as he turns from the interrogative to declarative back to interrogative mode—in a single sentence—his emphatic "*Must*," as well as his strained phrasing and ineffective punctuation, all seem to befuddle the poem's progression.

From Gray to Keats, from Poe to Dickinson, to a myriad of lesser "magazine poets," death was a favorite subject of the Romantics. Whitman's poem possesses no small portion of gothic morbidity. His tone is didactic and his diction is archaic, perhaps even a touch Quakerish (his mother, a strong influence, was Quaker), though occasionally he breaks into a cleaner and more contemporary phrasing. "This curious frame of human mould, / Where unrequited cravings play," for instance, anticipates tones and gestures of his later, great poems. He derives a clever doubleness from "mould," as the word signifies both a physical shape and the texture of decay.

But notice further that "curious frame" and those "unrequited cravings." In his 1856 "Sun-Down Poem" (recast as "Crossing Brooklyn

Ferry" in 1860), he wonders about the "curious" population in their evening commute. His curiosity suggests a subtle eroticism: Whitman wants contact, to be "fused" with "ever so many generations" of people. Physical union, in turn, provides for spiritual connectedness. "[C]urious abrupt questionings stir" there in Whitman's speaker, suggesting not only his passion for physical contact but his specifically homoerotic desire, embodied by the young men on the ferry-dock "leaning . . . their flesh against me." The "unrequited cravings" in "Time to Come" may be Whitman's first guarded intimations of homoerotic passion.

"Time to Come" initiates one of the great conundrums of Whitman's work, the problem of death: that is, the inevitability of death, the individual body's decay, and the soul's resulting dislocation. Because the body dies, the soul is imperiled as well, and the speaker's "struggling brain" remains admittedly "powerless" to propose any answer. The mournful tones express Whitman's metaphysical concern over a physical, bodily dilemma. Of course, he doesn't solve the problem in this poem. That will come later, in poems like "Crossing Brooklyn Ferry," "When Lilacs Last in the Dooryard Bloom'd," and "Song of Myself." In these poems he will resolve the problem of death by joining it, enlisting its aid, and returning reborn to the world singing a "victorious song, death's outlet song"—the transcendentalist's song of grief-turned-to-praise.

The distance between "Time to Come" and his later, great transcendental poems is thus substantial—in form, theme, and ambition. Before Walter Whitman becomes Walt, he must absorb Emerson. He must soak up the expansive grandeur of opera. He must study the rhetoric of the Bible. He must delight in the stump-speeches of local politicians. He must immerse himself in the life and language of working-class areas around Brooklyn and Manhattan. He must tend the broken bodies of soldiers at a hospital in Washington, D.C. And he must work out the scheme of his free-verse formulations. But already, in "Time to Come," he is asking the single most important question that will guide his greatest poems toward their ends.

The Mock Song

JOHN WILMOT, EARL OF ROCHESTER

"I swive as well as others do;
I'm young, not yet deform'd;
My tender heart, sincere and true,
Deserves not to be scorn'd.
Why, Phyllis, then, why will you swive
With forty lovers more?"
"Can I," she said, "with nature strive?
Alas I am, alas I am a whore!"

"Were all my body larded o'er
With darts of love, so thick
That you might find in every pore
A well-stuck standing prick,
Whilst yet my eyes alone were free,
My heart would never doubt,
In am'rous rage and ecstasie,
To wish those eyes, to wish those eyes fuckt out."

BARRY GOLDENSOHN ON JOHN WILMOT'S The Mock Song

As soon as courtly love and its rusticated cousin, the pastoral, be-
came the fashion, the English poetic tradition greeted their idealization
of love with an earthy mockery (bless its native empiricism!) that kept
the ideal and the debunking modes vibrating in tension. This is both a
tribute and a great service to the amplitude and variety of human sexu-
ality. Likewise, it is necessary and desirable for poets to redeem the art
of poetry from Emerson's romantic idealization, with its glorification of
sublimity and its contempt for wit. His essay defining "The Poet" ("the
man without impediment, who seeks and handles what others dream
of . . . a sovereign . . . a beholder of ideas, an utterer of the necessary,"
etc.) is remarkable for quoting no other poetry but seven didactic and
platonizing lines of Spencer, ending "For, of the soul, the body form
doth take, / For soul is form, and doth the body make."

Careful attention to our species suggests that the body has its own priorities, inclinations, demands, and so forth. Careful attention to poetry suggests that the art is wonderfully diverse, and the attitudes, tones, voices, methods, and simple human resources that it employs go well beyond what Emerson understands by the obligatory witless sublimity of great poetry. We must remind ourselves of other delights when we hear the seductive call of this spiritual megalomania that is so pervasive in our culture. Emerson didn't invent it.

Rochester's "Mock Song" glitters in the tradition of outrageous, hyperbolic wit, derived from Donne, that is comfortable with the outrageous and hyperbolic. It is written in response to the trite and silly courtly love poem, "I cannot change as others do," by Sir Carr Scroope, whose name survives only in footnotes as a target of satire. In Scroope's poem, he vows to die of grief as the way to his scornful lover's heart: "For such a faithful tender heart, / Can never break, can never break in vain." In Rochester's poem, we do not deal with possible actions of human bodies and sexual organs, but with a comic vision of the spiritual form of lust—more precisely, a male comic fantasy of female lust, natural, boundless, generous. The gleeful absurdity of the hyperbole, the exuberance which is its beauty, the energy which is its eternal delight, make the poem a celebration and not a satire. It is a vision of an impossible maleness with an impossible femaleness, which is C. S. Lewis' definition of lust. Underlying this vision are the feelings of transport of the erotic body: "I feel all prick, all cunt." And in the mouth of a female speaker, the conclusion of the poem is no more masochistic than the expression "I fucked my head off."

Textual Note: The poem was suppressed from all but the earliest collections of Rochester's work. I encountered it in a facsimile edition of *Poems on Several Occasions by the Right Honorable Earl of R——* that appeared in the year of his death, 1680, an exploitation volume that added many poems, most of them boringly obscene, to the core of work that can be attributed to Rochester. The facsimile was published by Princeton University Press in 1950, with careful though not always accurate notes by James Thorpe. The volume attributes the Scroope poem to Rochester, and since it contains a number of Aphra Behn's poems swept up by the original compiler in 1680, I took delight in the possibility that "Mock Song" could be her parody of Rochester. However, this possibility was scotched by the careful studies of attribution by David Vieth in the '60s. The ingenious Ms. Heather McHugh included the poem in an essay in the Jan/Feb 2002 issue of *The American Poetry Review,* which is undoubtedly the first appearance of the poem in a mass circulation magazine in the 330 years since it was written. I am glad to contribute to its rehabilitation.

Fromeréville
War in Heaven

JOHN ALLAN WYETH

A reek of steam—the bath-house rang with cries.
"Come across with the soap."
         "Like hell, what makes you think
it's yours?"
         "Don't turn *off the water,* that ain't fair
I'm all *covered* with soap."
         "Hurry up, get out of the way."
"Thank God you're takin' a bath."
         "He wants to surprise
us."
   "Oh is that so, well anyway I don't stink
like you."
   "Air raid!"
         We ran out into the square,
naked and cold like souls on Judgment Day.
Over us, white clouds blazoned on blue skies,
and a green balloon on fire—we watched it shrink
into flame and a fall of smoke. Around us, brute
guns belching puffs of shrapnel in the air,
where one plane swooping like a bird of prey
spat fire into a dangling parachute.

There are degrees of literary obscurity. The unjust neglect one writer suffers can seem like renown compared to the utter oblivion that besets another. Weldon Kees (1914–55) is obscure in that his remarkable poems still do not appear in many anthologies and remain unknown to most academic critics. Yet Kees's poetry has never been out of print since it was first collected in 1960, and he is fervently admired by many influential poets in both the U.S. and Europe. Radcliffe Squires (1917–93) is more obscure. His poetry appears in no current anthologies, and there is nothing published about his work beyond its initial reviews except a few remembrances written at the time of his death. Yet any curious reader with Internet access can quickly track down most of his seven volumes of verse and five critical books. He is unknown, therefore, but not unknowable.

The American poet John Allan Wyeth (1894–1980), however, is truly obscure. Compared to him, Kees is William Faulkner and Squires is John Crowe Ransom. Wyeth is not merely a forgotten poet. He was never noticed. Unmentioned in literary histories and critical literature even in his own lifetime, his work appears in no anthologies of any sort--not anywhere, not ever. Several years of research have turned up only a few scraps published about him—a yearbook photograph, three brief obituaries, two passing sentences in Edmund Wilson's journals, and a forty-three-word notice in *Poetry* (Dec. 1932). Why complain about such oblivion? However vast, the Lethean library always has room for more authors. The reason for my protest is simple: Wyeth is the finest American soldier-poet of World War I.

I take no credit for rediscovering Wyeth's poetry. All I did was recognize its excellence. I would never have seen his work had it not been for the military historian and poet Bradley Omanson, who asked my opinion of the author's work. Reading the photocopies that Omanson sent me, I felt both pleasure and surprise. Wyeth's poetry was not only vividly realized; it was unique. Cunningly combining traditional form and modernist methods, realistic narrative and imagistic lyricality, Wyeth was the missing man in the history of twentieth century American poetry—an important soldier-poet from the Great War.

Wyeth is not a major poet. His body of work is too small, and his literary ambitions too circumscribed. He lacks the tragic vision and mythic resonance of Wilfred Owen—or even the best of Siegfried Sassoon. But to define the limits of Wyeth's achievement is not to deny it. Although his poems have an almost documentary quality in their narrative details and language, they remain, seventy-five years after their publication, fresh and immediate in their impact. He is a powerfully expressive and distinctively individual poet.

There is nothing available on Wyeth or his work. Here are the facts of his life as I have been able to discover them, mostly from school records and family members. John Allan Wyeth Jr. was born in New York City, the third child of a noted surgeon. His father, John Allan Wyeth Sr., a former Confederate soldier and a published poet, was a founder of New York Polyclinic Hospital and Medical School. Wyeth attended the Lawrenceville School, a private preparatory school in New Jersey, where he was president of the drama club and class poet. In 1911, he entered Princeton, where his literary acquaintances included fellow undergraduate Edmund Wilson, who called Wyeth the "only aesthete" in the Class of 1915. After graduation, Wyeth went on to earn a master's degree from Princeton in 1917. He enlisted later that year in the army to fight in World War I. His fluent knowledge of French led him to an assignment in the Corps of Interpreters with the 33rd Division. By May, 1918, he was in France, and was soon involved in the late battles on the Somme and Verdun. Eventually the 33rd division became part of the Army of Occupation in Germany. Discharged in 1919, Wyeth taught French at St. Paul's school before quitting to become a painter. In 1932 he began studying with the English painter Duncan Grant. He achieved enough success to have his work exhibited at the Corcoran Gallery in Washington. He spent much of his life in Europe, though he served in the U.S. Coast Guard during World War II. He resettled permanently in the United States in later life and converted to Catholicism. He never married. (He was almost certainly gay.) He died at age eighty-six in Princeton.

Wyeth's literary importance rests solely on one remarkable book of poems, *This Man's Army: A War In Fifty-Odd Sonnets* (1928). This striking, naturalistic sonnet sequence chronicles the movements of an American troop division, from receiving sailing orders and disembarkation in France through the battles across the Western front. Using slangy dialogue and vivid description, the poems present the war in brief, memorable scenes. Each sonnet begins by creating a narrative scene but ultimately rises to a lyrical conclusion. Wyeth's poems are also technically innovative. For the book-length sequence, he created a new rhyme scheme based on the Petrarchan sonnet, but better adapted to the paucity of English-language rhymes.

While formal, Wyeth's language is as fresh, varied, and contemporary as that of most free-verse poets of the period. The syntax alternates between provocative fragments and direct narration. There are no inversions, forced rhymes, or stale diction. (Most of the poetry by our soldiers was written in a traditional Romantic style—as in Alan Seegar's "I Have a Rendezvous with Death.") Wyeth's sonnets have the narrative vitality and stark realism of prose but with the concision and lyricism of poetry. There is nothing quite like *This Man's Army* elsewhere in modern American poetry. Taken as a whole, the sequence is comparable in scope and quality to the best British poetry from the Great War. Long forgotten, it deserves careful reassessment. Wyeth never wrote another volume of poetry. *This Man's Army* is out of print.

"A Bookshop Idyll" by Kingsley Amis is reprinted by kind permission of Jonathan Clowes Ltd., London, on behalf of the Literary Estate of Kingsley Amis. Copyright © 1957 Kingsley Amis.

"New Years Poem" by Margaret Avison from *Always Now: The Collected Poems* (Porcupine's Quill, 2003) is reprinted with the kind permission of The Porcupine's Quill Inc.

David Baker's essay on Walt Whitman's "Time to Come" first appeared in *The New England Review* and is reprinted here with the permission of the author.

"Morfudd's Hair" by Edward Barrett is reprinted with the permission of the poet.

"Young Woman's Song" from *Collected Poems: 1937–1971* by John Berryman, © 1989 by Kate Donahue Berryman. Reprinted by permission of Farrar, Straus and Giroux, LLC.

"Poem" from *The Complete Poems 1927–1979* by Elizabeth Bishop. © 1979, 1983 by Alice Helen Methfessel. Reprinted by permission of Farrar, Straus and Giroux, LLC.

"Mirage" by R. P. Blackmur from *Poems of R. P. Blackmur*. Copyright © 1977 Princeton University Press, 2005 renewed PUP. Reprinted by permission of Princeton University Press.

"Old Countryside" from *The Blue Estuaries* by Louise Bogan, © 1968 by Louise Bogan. Copyright renewed 1996 by Ruth Limmer. Reprinted by permission of Farrar, Straus and Giroux LLC.

"Drunken Winter" by Joseph Ceravolo from *The Green Lake is Awake* (Coffee House Press, 1994), is reprinted by permission of Coffee House Press.

"A Trenta Sei of the Pleasure We Take in the Early Death of Keats" by John Ciardi is reprinted by kind permission of the Ciardi Family Trust.

"Whatever Happened to Don Ho" by Tom Clark, © Tom Clark. Reprinted by kind permission of the poet.

"This world is not conclusion" and "A Pit—but Heaven over it" from *The Poems of Emily Dickinson,* Thomas H. Johnson, ed., Cambridge, Mass.: The Belknap

BETTY ADCOCK's most recent book is *Intervale: New and Selected Poems* (Louisiana State University Press, 2001), co-winner of the Poets' Prize. She was a Guggenheim Fellow in 2002–2003 and currently is writer-in-residence at Meredith College and a faculty member at the Warren Wilson MFA Program for Writers.

PAMELA ALEXANDER is the author of *Inland*, winner of the 1997 Iowa Poetry Prize, *Commonwealth of Wings* (Wesleyan, 1991), and *Navigable Waterways*, winner of the 1985 Yale Younger Poets series. She is one of the editors of *FIELD*.

MAGGIE ANDERSON's most recent book is *Windfall: New and Selected Poems*. She directs the Wick Poetry Center and edits the Wick Poetry Series at Kent State University.

RAE ARMANTROUT's latest books are *It's Up To Speed* (Wesleyan, 2004) and *Veil: New and Selected Poems* (Wesleyan, 2001).

JOHN ASHBERY has been the recipient of the Pulitzer Prize, the National Book Award, and the National Book Critics Circle Award. His most recent book is *Where Shall I Wander* (Ecco Press, 2005).

DAVID BAKER's newest books are *Midwest Ecologue* (W. W. Norton, 2005) and *Treatise on Touch: Selected Poems* (Arc Publications, U.K., 2005).

MARY JO BANG is a contributing editor to *Boston Review*. Her latest books are *The Eye like a Strange Balloon* (Grove, 2004) and *Louise in Love* (Grove, 2001).

CHARLES BERNSTEIN's newest books are *With Strings* (University of Chicago Press, 2001) and *Republics of Reality: 1975–1995* (Sun & Moon Press, 2000).

LINDA BIERDS is the author of *First Hand* and *The Seconds*, both from Putnam, and *The Profile Makers* (Holt, 1997), among others.

DON BOGEN is the author of *The Known World* and *After the Splendid Display,* both from Wesleyan University Press. His newest collection is *Luster* (Wesleyan, 2003). He teaches at the University of Cincinnati.

CHRISTOPHER BUCKLEY is the author of many books, the most recent of which are *A Condition of the Spirit: On the Life and Work of Larry Levis* (Eastern Washington University Press, 2004) and *Sky* (Sheep Meadow, 2004).

NICK CARBÓ's books are *El Grupo McDonalds* and *Secret Asian Man,* both from Tia Chucha Press.

WANDA COLEMAN's newest book is *Ostinato Vamps* (Pitt Poetry Series, 2003). Her book *Mercurochrome* (Black Sparrow) was a bronze-medal finalist for the National Book Award (2001).

BILLY COLLINS served as U.S. Poet Laureate from 2001 to 2003. His newest books are *The Trouble with Poetry and Other Poems*, *Nine Horses*, and *Sailing Alone Around the Room,* all published by Random House.

MARTHA COLLINS is the author of *Blue Front* (Graywolf, 2006), among others. She is one of the editors of *FIELD.*

JIM DANIELS' most recent books are *Show and Tell: New and Selected Poems* (University of Wisconsin Press, 2003) and *Detroit Tales: Stories* (Michigan State University Press, 2003).

TOI DERRICOTTE is the author of *The Black Notebooks: An Interior Journey* (Norton, 1999) and *Tender* (University of Pittsburgh Press, 1997).

DENISE DUHAMEL's *Queen for a Day: New and Selected Poems* appeared from the University of Pittsburgh Press in 2001.

LYNN EMANUEL's newest book is *Then, Suddenly* (University of Pittsburgh Press, 1999).

ANNIE FINCH is the author of *Calendars* (Tupelo, 2003) and *Eve* (Story Line, 1997).

RICHARD FOERSTER's newest books are *Double Going* (2002) and *Trillium* (1998), both published by BOA Editions. Forthcoming is *The Burning of Troy* (BOA, 2006).

AMY GERSTLER's *Ghost Girl* was published in 2004 by Penguin Press. Carnegie Mellon University Press reissued her *Bitter Angel,* which won the 1991 National Book Critics Circle Award.

DANA GIOIA is Chairman of the National Endowment for the Arts. He is also author, most recently, of *Disappearing Ink* (Graywolf, 2004) and *Interrogations at Noon* (Graywolf, 2001).

PETER GIZZI's books include *Some Values of Landscape and Weather* (Wesleyan, 2003) and *Artificial Heart* (Burning Deck, 1998). He is also the editor of *The House That Jack Built: The Collected Lectures of Jack Spicer* (Wesleyan, 1998).

ELTON GLASER has published six full-length collections of poems, most recently *Here and Hereafter* (Arkansas, 2005) and *Pelican Tracks* (Southern Illinois, 2003).

ALBERT GOLDBARTH has twice received the National Book Critics Circle Award. His newest book is *Budget Travel Through Space and Time* (Graywolf, 2005).

BARRY GOLDENSOHN is the author of *Dance Music* (The Cummington Press, 1992) and *The Marrano* (National Poetry Foundation, 1988).

MARILYN HACKER's newest books are *Desesperanto: Poems 1999–2002* (Norton, 2003) and *Squares and Courtyards: Poems* (Norton, 2000).

RACHEL HADAS is the author of *Laws* (Zoo, 2004), *Indelible* (Wesleyan, 2001), and *Halfway Down the Hall: New and Selected Poems* (Wesleyan, 1998), among others.

FORREST HAMER is the author of *Middle Ear* (California Poetry Series, 2000) and *Call & Response* (Alice James Books, 1995).

TONY HOAGLAND's books are *What Narcissism Means to Me* (Graywolf, 2003), *Donkey Gospel* (Graywolf, 1998), and *Sweet Ruin* (University of Wisconsin Press, 1993).

JOHN HOLLANDER's latest books are *Picture Windows* (Knopf, 2003) and *Figurehead and Other Poems* (Knopf, 2000).

FANNY HOWE's recent books are *Gone: Poems* (University of California Press, 2003) and *Selected Poems* (University of California Press, 2000).

CAROLYN KIZER's most recent book is *Cool, Calm, and Collected: Poems 1960–2000* (Copper Canyon Press, 2003). She received the 1985 Pulitzer Prize for poetry.

JOHN KOETHE's *North Point North: New and Selected Poems* appeared in 2002 from HarperCollins, who will publish his new collection, *Sally's Hair*.

DAVID LEHMAN's recent books include *When a Woman Loves a Man* (Scribner, 2005), *The Evening Sun* (Scribner, 2002), and *The Last Avant-Garde: The Making of the New York School of Poets*. He is preparing a new edition of *The Oxford Book of American Poetry*.

SUSAN LUDVIGSON's new collection, *Escaping the House of Certainty*, is due to appear from LSU Press in 2006. Her book *Sweet Confluence: New and Selected Poems* was published by LSU Press in 2001.

J. D. MCCLATCHY is editor of *The Vintage Book of Contemporary American Poetry* and author of *American Writers at Home* (Knopf, 2004) and *Hazmat* (Knopf, 2002), among many others. He is also editor of *The Yale Review*.

PAUL MULDOON's most recent books are *Moy Sand and Gravel* (Farrar Straus & Giroux, 2002) and *Poems 1968–1998* (Farrar Straus & Giroux, 2001).

CAROL MUSKE-DUKES' most recent books are *Sparrow* (Random House, 2003), *Married to the Ice Pick Killer* (Random House, 2002), *Life After Death* (Random House, 2001), and *An Octave Above Thunder: New and Selected Poems* (Penguin, 1997).

HOA NGUYEN edits *Skanky Possum* with her husband, Dale Smith. She is author, most recently, of *Red Juice* (Effing Press) and *Your Ancient See Through* (Subpress).

ERIC PANKEY's most recent books are *Reliquaries* (Ausable, 2005), *Oracle Figures* (Ausable, 2003), and *Cenotaph* (Knopf, 2001).

ALAN MICHAEL PARKER's newest books are *Cry Uncle* (University of Mississippi Press, 2005) and *Love Song with Motor Vehicles* (BOA Editions, 2003). He is also editor of the *Routledge Anthology of Cross Gendered Verse* (1996).

ELISE PASCHEN is the co-editor of *Poetry in Motion from Coast to Coast* (Norton, 2002) and *Poetry Speaks* (Sourcebooks, 2001). She is also the author of *Infidelities* (Story Line Press, 1996).

MOLLY PEACOCK's newest book is *Cornucopia: New and Selected Poems* (Norton, 2002). She is a member of the Graduate Faculty of Spalding University's Brief Residency MFA Program.

LUCIA PERILLO's most recent book is *The Oldest Map with the Name North America* (Random House, 1999). She was a 2000 MacArthur Fellow.

CARL PHILLIPS' most recent books are *The Rest of Love* (Farrar, Straus and Giroux, 2004) and *Coin of the Realm: Essays on the Life and Art of Poetry* (Graywolf, 2004).

ROBERT PHILLIPS' newest books are *The Madness of Art: Interviews with Poets and Writers* (Syracuse, 2003) and *Spinach Days* (Johns Hopkins, 2001).

STANLEY PLUMLY's book of essays, *Argument & Song: Sources and Silences in Poetry*, appeared from Handsel Books in 2003. *Now That My Father Lies Down Beside Me: New and Selected Poems, 1970–2000* was published by Ecco Press in 2001.

D. A. POWELL is author of *Cocktails* (Graywolf, 2004), *Lunch* (Wesleyan University Press, 2001), and *Tea* (Wesleyan University Press, 1998).

BIN RAMKE's newest books are *Matter* (University of Iowa Press, 2004), *Airs, Waters, Places* (University of Iowa Press, 2001), *Wake* (University of Iowa Press, 1999), and *Massacre of the Innocents* (University of Iowa Press, 1995). He is editor of *Denver Quarterly.*

LLOYD SCHWARTZ's books are *Cairo Traffic* (University of Chicago Press, 2000) and *Goodnight, Gracie* (1992), among others. He received the Pulitzer Prize for criticism in 1994.

REGINALD SHEPHERD's books are *Otherhood, Wrong, Angel, Interrupted,* and *Some Are Drowning,* all from the University of Pittsburgh Press.

DALE SMITH edits *Skanky Possum* with his wife, Hoa Nguyen. He is the author, most recently, of *Notes No Answer* (Habenicht) and *The Flood + the Garden* (First Intensity, 2002).

R. T. SMITH's newest books are *The Hollow Log Lounge* (University of Illinois Press, 2003) and *Messenger* (Louisiana State University Press, 2001). He is editor of *Shenandoah: The Washington and Lee University Review.*

DAVID ST. JOHN's newest books are *Prism* (Arctos Press, 2002) and *The Red Leaves of Night* (Harper Perennial, 2000). He also edited *The Selected Levis* (University of Pittsburgh Press, 2002).

COLE SWENSEN is author of *Such Rich Hour* (University of Iowa Press, 2001), *Try* (University of Iowa Press, 1999), which won the Iowa Poetry Prize; *Noon* (Sun & Moon Press, 1998); *Numen* (Burning Deck, 1995); and *New Math,* winner of the National Poetry Series. She has translated four books of poetry from the French.

ANN TOWNSEND's new collection of poems is *The Coronary Garden* (Sarabande Books, 2005). Her *Dime Store Erotics* (Silverfish Review Press, 1998) won the 1997 Gerald Cable Award.

DAVID TRINIDAD's books are *Plasticville* (Turtle Point, 2000) and *Hand Over Heart: Poems 1981–1988* (Amethyst, 1991), among others.

RACHEL WETZSTEON's books are *Sakura Park* (Persea, 2006), *Influential Ghosts: A Study of Auden's Sources* (Routledge, 2005), *Home and Away* (Penguin, 1998), and *The Other Stars* (Penguin, 1994), winner of the National Poetry Series.

SUSAN WHEELER's books of poetry are *Ledger* (University of Iowa Press, 2005), *Source Codes* (Salt, 2001), *Smokes* (Four Way Books, 1998), and *Bag O' Diamonds* (University of Georgia Press, 1994). Her novel, *Record Palace*, was published by Graywolf in 2005.

DARA WIER's books are *Reverse Rapture* (Verse, 2005), *Hat on a Pond* (Verse, 2002), *Voyages in English* (Carnegie Mellon, 2001), and *Our Master Plan* (Carnegie Mellon, 1999), among others.

C. K. WILLIAMS' newest books are *The Singing* (Farrar, Straus and Giroux, 2003), winner of the National Book Award; *Misgivings: My Mother, My Father, Myself* (Farrar, Straus and Giroux, 2001); *Love About Love* (Ausable, 2001); and *Repair* (Farrar, Straus and Giroux, 1999), winner of the 2000 Pulitzer Prize.

MILLER WILLIAMS' newest books are *The Lives of Kevin Fletcher* (University of Georgia Press, 2002) and *Some Jazz a While: Collected Poems* (University of Illinois Press, 1999).

DAVID WOJAHN's most recent books are *Spirit Cabinet* (University of Pittsburgh Press, 2002), *Strange Good Fortune: Essays on Contemporary Poetry* (University of Arkansas Press, 2001), and *The Falling Hour* (University of Pittsburgh Press, 1997).

STEPHEN YENSER's books are *A Boundless Field: American Poetry at Large* (University of Michigan Press, 2002) and *The Fire in All Things* (Louisiana State University Press, 1993), among others.

DEAN YOUNG's newest books are *Elegy on a Toy Piano* (University of Pittsburgh Press, 2005) and *Skid* (University of Pittsburgh Press, 2002).

THE UNIVERSITY OF ILLINOIS PRESS

IS A FOUNDING MEMBER OF THE

ASSOCIATION OF AMERICAN UNIVERSITY PRESSES.

COMPOSED IN 11/13 ADOBE GARAMOND

WITH KAUFMANN AND FUTURA DISPLAY

BY JIM PROEFROCK

AT THE UNIVERSITY OF ILLINOIS PRESS

DESIGNED BY COPENHAVER CUMPSTON

MANUFACTURED BY THOMSON-SHORE, INC.

University of Illinois Press

1325 SOUTH OAK STREET   CHAMPAIGN, IL 61820-6903

WWW.PRESS.UILLINOIS.EDU